DICTIONARY
THEME–BASED

British English Collection

ENGLISH-
AFRIKAANS

The most useful words
To expand your lexicon and sharpen
your language skills

7000 words

Theme-based dictionary British English-Afrikaans - 7000 words

By Andrey Taranov

T&P Books vocabularies are intended for helping you learn, memorize and review foreign words. The dictionary is divided into themes, covering all major spheres of everyday activities, business, science, culture, etc.

The process of learning words using T&P Books' theme-based dictionaries gives you the following advantages:

- Correctly grouped source information predetermines success at subsequent stages of word memorization
- Availability of words derived from the same root allowing memorization of word units (rather than separate words)
- Small units of words facilitate the process of establishing associative links needed for consolidation of vocabulary
- Level of language knowledge can be estimated by the number of learned words

T&P Books Publishing
www.tpbooks.com

This book is also available in E-book formats.
Please visit www.tpbooks.com or the major online bookstores.

AFRIKAANS THEME-BASED DICTIONARY
British English collection

T&P Books vocabularies are intended to help you learn, memorize, and review foreign words. The vocabulary contains over 7000 commonly used words arranged thematically.

- Vocabulary contains the most commonly used words
- Recommended as an addition to any language course
- Meets the needs of beginners and advanced learners of foreign languages
- Convenient for daily use, revision sessions, and self-testing activities
- Allows you to assess your vocabulary

Special features of the vocabulary

- Words are organized according to their meaning, not alphabetically
- Words are presented in three columns to facilitate the reviewing and self-testing processes
- Words in groups are divided into small blocks to facilitate the learning process
- The vocabulary offers a convenient and simple transcription of each foreign word

The vocabulary has 198 topics including:

Basic Concepts, Numbers, Colors, Months, Seasons, Units of Measurement, Clothing & Accessories, Food & Nutrition, Restaurant, Family Members, Relatives, Character, Feelings, Emotions, Diseases, City, Town, Sightseeing, Shopping, Money, House, Home, Office, Working in the Office, Import & Export, Marketing, Job Search, Sports, Education, Computer, Internet, Tools, Nature, Countries, Nationalities and more ...

TABLE OF CONTENTS

PRONUNCIATION GUIDE

T&P phonetic alphabet	Afrikaans example	English example
[a]	land	shorter than in 'ask'
[ã]	straat	calf, palm
[æ]	hout	chess, man
[o], [ɔ]	Australië	drop, baught
[e]	metaal	elm, medal
[ɛ]	aanlê	man, bad
[ə]	filter	driver, teacher
[ɪ]	uur	big, America
[i]	billik	shorter than in 'feet'
[ĩ]	naïef	tree, big
[o]	koppie	pod, John
[ø]	akteur	eternal, church
[œ]	fluit	German Hölle
[u]	hulle	book
[ʊ]	hout	good, booklet
[b]	bakker	baby, book
[d]	donder	day, doctor
[f]	navraag	face, food
[g]	burger	game, gold
[h]	driehoek	home, have
[j]	byvoeg	yes, New York
[k]	kamera	clock, kiss
[l]	loon	lace, people
[m]	môre	magic, milk
[n]	neef	sang, thing
[p]	pyp	pencil, private
[r]	rigting	rice, radio
[s]	oplos	city, boss
[t]	lood, tenk	tourist, trip
[v]	bewaar	very, river
[w]	oorwinnaar	vase, winter
[z]	zoem	zebra, please
[dʒ]	enjin	joke, general
[ʃ]	artisjok	machine, shark
[ŋ]	kans	English, ring
[tʃ]	tjek	church, French
[ʒ]	beige	forge, pleasure
[x]	agent	as in Scots 'loch'

ABBREVIATIONS
used in the dictionary

English abbreviations

ab.	-	about
adj	-	adjective
adv	-	adverb
anim.	-	animate
as adj	-	attributive noun used as adjective
e.g.	-	for example
etc.	-	et cetera
fam.	-	familiar
fem.	-	feminine
form.	-	formal
inanim.	-	inanimate
masc.	-	masculine
math	-	mathematics
mil.	-	military
n	-	noun
pl	-	plural
pron.	-	pronoun
sb	-	somebody
sing.	-	singular
sth	-	something
v aux	-	auxiliary verb
vi	-	intransitive verb
vi, vt	-	intransitive, transitive verb
vt	-	transitive verb

BASIC CONCEPTS

Basic concepts. Part 1

1. Pronouns

I, me	**ek, my**	[ɛk], [maj]
you	**jy**	[jaj]
he	**hy**	[haj]
she	**sy**	[saj]
it	**dit**	[dit]
we	**ons**	[ɔŋs]
you (to a group)	**julle**	[jullə]
you (polite, sing.)	**u**	[u]
you (polite, pl)	**u**	[u]
they	**hulle**	[hullə]

2. Greetings. Salutations. Farewells

Hello! (fam.)	**Hallo!**	[hallo!]
Hello! (form.)	**Hallo!**	[hallo!]
Good morning!	**Goeie môre!**	[χuje mɔrə!]
Good afternoon!	**Goeiemiddag!**	[χuje·middaχ!]
Good evening!	**Goeienaand!**	[χuje·nãnt!]
to say hello	**dagsê**	[daχsɛ:]
Hi! (hello)	**Hallo!**	[hallo!]
greeting (n)	**groet**	[χrut]
to greet (vt)	**groet**	[χrut]
How are you?	**Hoe gaan dit?**	[hu χãn dit?]
What's new?	**Hoe gaan dit?**	[hu χãn dit?]
Goodbye!	**Totsiens!**	[totsiŋs!]
Bye!	**Koebaai!**	[kubãi!]
See you soon!	**Totsiens!**	[totsiŋs!]
Farewell!	**Totsiens!**	[totsiŋs!]
Farewell! (to a friend)	**Mooi loop!**	[moj loəp!]
Farewell! (form.)	**Vaarwel!**	[fãrwel!]
to say goodbye	**afskeid neem**	[afskæjt neəm]
Cheers!	**Koebaai!**	[kubãi!]
Thank you! Cheers!	**Dankie!**	[danki!]
Thank you very much!	**Baie dankie!**	[baje danki!]
My pleasure!	**Plesier**	[plesir]
Don't mention it!	**Plesier!**	[plesir!]
It was nothing	**Plesier**	[plesir]

Excuse me! (fam.)	Ekskuus!	[ɛkskɪs!]
Excuse me! (form.)	Verskoon my!	[ferskoən maj!]
to excuse (forgive)	verskoon	[ferskoən]
to apologize (vi)	verskoning vra	[ferskoniŋ fra]
My apologies	Verskoning	[ferskoniŋ]
I'm sorry!	Ek is jammer!	[ɛk is jammər!]
to forgive (vt)	vergewe	[ferχevə]
It's okay! (that's all right)	Maak nie saak nie!	[māk ni sāk ni!]
please (adv)	asseblief	[asseblif]
Don't forget!	Vergeet dit nie!	[ferχeət dit ni!]
Certainly!	Beslis!	[beslis!]
Of course not!	Natuurlik nie!	[natɪrlik ni!]
Okay! (I agree)	OK!	[okej!]
That's enough!	Dis genoeg!	[dis χenuχ!]

3. Cardinal numbers. Part 1

0 zero	nul	[nul]
1 one	een	[eən]
2 two	twee	[weə]
3 three	drie	[dri]
4 four	vier	[fir]
5 five	vyf	[fajf]
6 six	ses	[ses]
7 seven	sewe	[sevə]
8 eight	ag	[aχ]
9 nine	nege	[neχə]
10 ten	tien	[tin]
11 eleven	elf	[ɛlf]
12 twelve	twaalf	[twālf]
13 thirteen	dertien	[dertin]
14 fourteen	veertien	[feərtin]
15 fifteen	vyftien	[fajftin]
16 sixteen	sestien	[sestin]
17 seventeen	sewetien	[sevətin]
18 eighteen	agtien	[aχtin]
19 nineteen	negetien	[neχetin]
20 twenty	twintig	[twintəχ]
21 twenty-one	een-en-twintig	[eən-en-twintəχ]
22 twenty-two	twee-en-twintig	[tweə-en-twintəχ]
23 twenty-three	drie-en-twintig	[dri-en-twintəχ]
30 thirty	dertig	[dertəχ]
31 thirty-one	een-en-dertig	[eən-en-dertəχ]
32 thirty-two	twee-en-dertig	[tweə-en-dertəχ]
33 thirty-three	drie-en-dertig	[dri-en-dertəχ]
40 forty	veertig	[feərtəχ]
41 forty-one	een-en-veertig	[eən-en-feərtəχ]

42 forty-two	**twee-en-veertig**	[twee-en-feertəx]
43 forty-three	**vier-en-veertig**	[fir-en-feertəx]
50 fifty	**vyftig**	[fajftəx]
51 fifty-one	**een-en-vyftig**	[een-en-fajftəx]
52 fifty-two	**twee-en-vyftig**	[twee-en-fajftəx]
53 fifty-three	**drie-en-vyftig**	[dri-en-fajftəx]
60 sixty	**sestig**	[sestəx]
61 sixty-one	**een-en-sestig**	[een-en-sestəx]
62 sixty-two	**twee-en-sestig**	[twee-en-sestəx]
63 sixty-three	**drie-en-sestig**	[dri-en-sestəx]
70 seventy	**sewentig**	[seventəx]
71 seventy-one	**een-en-sewentig**	[een-en-seventəx]
72 seventy-two	**twee-en-sewentig**	[twee-en-seventəx]
73 seventy-three	**drie-en-sewentig**	[dri-en-seventəx]
80 eighty	**tagtig**	[taχtəx]
81 eighty-one	**een-en-tagtig**	[een-en-taχtəx]
82 eighty-two	**twee-en-tagtig**	[twee-en-taχtəx]
83 eighty-three	**drie-en-tagtig**	[dri-en-taχtəx]
90 ninety	**negentig**	[neχentəx]
91 ninety-one	**een-en-negentig**	[een-en-neχentəx]
92 ninety-two	**twee-en-negentig**	[twee-en-neχentəx]
93 ninety-three	**drie-en-negentig**	[dri-en-neχentəx]

4. Cardinal numbers. Part 2

100 one hundred	**honderd**	[hondərt]
200 two hundred	**tweehonderd**	[twee·hondərt]
300 three hundred	**driehonderd**	[dri·hondərt]
400 four hundred	**vierhonderd**	[fir·hondərt]
500 five hundred	**vyfhonderd**	[fajf·hondərt]
600 six hundred	**seshonderd**	[ses·hondərt]
700 seven hundred	**sewehonderd**	[seve·hondərt]
800 eight hundred	**aghonderd**	[aχ·hondərt]
900 nine hundred	**negehonderd**	[neχe·hondərt]
1000 one thousand	**duisend**	[dœisent]
2000 two thousand	**tweeduisend**	[twee·dœisent]
3000 three thousand	**drieduisend**	[dri·dœisent]
10000 ten thousand	**tienduisend**	[tin·dœisent]
one hundred thousand	**honderdduisend**	[hondərt·dajsent]
million	**miljoen**	[miljun]
billion	**miljard**	[miljart]

5. Numbers. Fractions

fraction	**breuk**	[brøək]
one half	**helfte**	[hɛlftə]

| one third | derde | [derdə] |
| one quarter | kwart | [kwart] |

| one eighth | agste | [aχstə] |
| one tenth | tiende | [tində] |

| two thirds | twee derde | [tweə derdə] |
| three quarters | driekwart | [drikwart] |

6. Numbers. Basic operations

subtraction	aftrekking	[aftrɛkkiŋ]
to subtract (vi, vt)	aftrek	[aftrek]
division	deling	[deliŋ]
to divide (vt)	deel	[deəl]

addition	optelling	[optɛlliŋ]
to add up (vt)	optel	[optəl]
to add (vi)	optel	[optəl]
multiplication	vermenigvuldiging	[fermeniχ·fuldəχiŋ]
to multiply (vt)	vermenigvuldig	[fermeniχ·fuldəχ]

7. Numbers. Miscellaneous

digit, figure	syfer	[sajfər]
number	nommer	[nommər]
numeral	telwoord	[tɛlwoərt]
minus sign	minusteken	[minus·tekən]
plus sign	plusteken	[plus·tekən]
formula	formule	[formulə]

calculation	berekening	[berekeniŋ]
to count (vi, vt)	tel	[təl]
to count up	optel	[optəl]
to compare (vt)	vergelyk	[ferχəlajk]

| How much? | Hoeveel? | [hufeəl?] |
| How many? | Hoeveel? | [hufeəl?] |

sum, total	som, totaal	[som], [totāl]
result	resultaat	[resultāt]
remainder	oorskot	[oərskot]

little (I had ~ time)	min	[min]
few (I have ~ friends)	min	[min]
the rest	die res	[di res]
dozen	dosyn	[dosajn]

in half (adv)	middeldeur	[middəldøər]
equally (evenly)	gelyk	[χelajk]
half	helfte	[hɛlftə]
time (three ~s)	maal	[māl]

8. The most important verbs. Part 1

to advise (vt)	aanraai	[ānrāi]
to agree (say yes)	saamstem	[sāmstem]
to answer (vi, vt)	antwoord	[antwoərt]
to apologize (vi)	verskoning vra	[ferskoniŋ fra]
to arrive (vi)	aankom	[ānkom]
to ask (~ oneself)	vra	[fra]
to ask (~ sb to do sth)	vra	[fra]
to be (vi)	wees	[veəs]
to be afraid	bang wees	[baŋ veəs]
to be hungry	honger wees	[hoŋər veəs]
to be interested in ...	belangstel in ...	[belaŋstəl in ...]
to be needed	nodig wees	[nodəχ veəs]
to be surprised	verbaas wees	[ferbās veəs]
to be thirsty	dors wees	[dors veəs]
to begin (vt)	begin	[beχin]
to belong to ...	behoort aan ...	[behoərt ān ...]
to boast (vi)	spog	[spoχ]
to break (split into pieces)	breek	[breək]
to call (~ for help)	roep	[rup]
can (v aux)	kan	[kan]
to catch (vt)	vang	[faŋ]
to change (vt)	verander	[ferandər]
to choose (select)	kies	[kis]
to come down (the stairs)	afkom	[afkom]
to compare (vt)	vergelyk	[ferχəlajk]
to complain (vi, vt)	kla	[kla]
to confuse (mix up)	verwar	[ferwar]
to continue (vt)	aangaan	[āŋχān]
to control (vt)	kontroleer	[kontroleər]
to cook (dinner)	kook	[koək]
to cost (vt)	kos	[kos]
to count (add up)	tel	[təl]
to count on ...	reken op ...	[reken op ...]
to create (vt)	skep	[skep]
to cry (weep)	huil	[hœil]

9. The most important verbs. Part 2

to deceive (vi, vt)	bedrieg	[bedrəχ]
to decorate (tree, street)	versier	[fersir]
to defend (a country, etc.)	verdedig	[ferdedəχ]
to demand (request firmly)	eis	[æjs]
to dig (vt)	grawe	[χravə]
to discuss (vt)	bespreek	[bespreək]
to do (vt)	doen	[dun]

to doubt (have doubts)	**twyfel**	[twajfəl]
to drop (let fall)	**laat val**	[lãt fal]
to enter (room, house, etc.)	**binnegaan**	[binnəχãn]
to excuse (forgive)	**verskoon**	[ferskoən]
to exist (vi)	**bestaan**	[bestãn]
to expect (foresee)	**voorsien**	[foərsin]
to explain (vt)	**verduidelik**	[ferdœidəlik]
to fall (vi)	**val**	[fal]
to fancy (vt)	**hou van**	[hæʊ fan]
to find (vt)	**vind**	[fint]
to finish (vt)	**klaarmaak**	[klãrmãk]
to fly (vi)	**vlieg**	[fliχ]
to follow … (come after)	**volg …**	[folχ …]
to forget (vi, vt)	**vergeet**	[ferχeət]
to forgive (vt)	**vergewe**	[ferχevə]
to give (vt)	**gee**	[χeə]
to go (on foot)	**gaan**	[χãn]
to go for a swim	**gaan swem**	[χãn swem]
to go out (for dinner, etc.)	**uitgaan**	[œitχãn]
to guess (the answer)	**raai**	[rãi]
to have (vt)	**hê**	[hɛ:]
to have breakfast	**ontbyt**	[ontbajt]
to have dinner	**aandete gebruik**	[ãndetə χebrœik]
to have lunch	**gaan eet**	[χãn eət]
to hear (vt)	**hoor**	[hoər]
to help (vt)	**help**	[hɛlp]
to hide (vt)	**wegsteek**	[veχsteək]
to hope (vi, vt)	**hoop**	[hoəp]
to hunt (vi, vt)	**jag**	[jaχ]
to hurry (vi)	**opskud**	[opskut]

10. The most important verbs. Part 3

to inform (vt)	**in kennis stel**	[in kɛnnis stəl]
to insist (vi, vt)	**aandring**	[ãndriŋ]
to insult (vt)	**beledig**	[beledəχ]
to invite (vt)	**uitnooi**	[œitnoj]
to joke (vi)	**grappies maak**	[χrappis mãk]
to keep (vt)	**bewaar**	[bevãr]
to keep silent, to hush	**stilbly**	[stilblaj]
to kill (vt)	**doodmaak**	[doədmãk]
to know (sb)	**ken**	[ken]
to know (sth)	**weet**	[veət]
to laugh (vi)	**lag**	[laχ]
to liberate (city, etc.)	**bevry**	[befraj]
to look for … (search)	**soek …**	[suk …]

| to love (sb) | liefhê | [lifhɛ:] |
| to manage, to run | beheer | [beheər] |

to mean (signify)	beteken	[betekən]
to mention (talk about)	verwys na	[ferwajs na]
to miss (school, etc.)	bank	[bank]
to notice (see)	raaksien	[rāksin]
to object (vi, vt)	beswaar maak	[beswār māk]

to observe (see)	waarneem	[vārneəm]
to open (vt)	oopmaak	[oəpmāk]
to order (meal, etc.)	bestel	[bestəl]
to order (mil.)	beveel	[befeəl]
to own (possess)	besit	[besit]

to participate (vi)	deelneem	[deəlneəm]
to pay (vi, vt)	betaal	[betāl]
to permit (vt)	toestaan	[tustān]
to plan (vt)	beplan	[beplan]
to play (children)	speel	[speəl]

to pray (vi, vt)	bid	[bit]
to prefer (vt)	verkies	[ferkis]
to promise (vt)	beloof	[beloəf]
to pronounce (vt)	uitspreek	[œitspreək]
to propose (vt)	voorstel	[foərstəl]
to punish (vt)	straf	[straf]

11. The most important verbs. Part 4

to read (vi, vt)	lees	[leəs]
to recommend (vt)	aanbeveel	[ānbefeəl]
to refuse (vi, vt)	weier	[væjer]
to regret (be sorry)	jammer wees	[jammər veəs]
to rent (sth from sb)	huur	[hɪr]

to repeat (say again)	herhaal	[herhāl]
to reserve, to book	bespreek	[bespreək]
to run (vi)	hardloop	[hardloəp]
to save (rescue)	red	[ret]

to say (~ thank you)	sê	[sɛ:]
to scold (vt)	uitvaar teen	[œitfār teən]
to see (vt)	sien	[sin]
to sell (vt)	verkoop	[ferkoəp]

to send (vt)	stuur	[stɪr]
to shoot (vi)	skiet	[skit]
to shout (vi)	skreeu	[skriʋ]
to show (vt)	wys	[vajs]
to sign (document)	teken	[tekən]

| to sit down (vi) | gaan sit | [χān sit] |
| to smile (vi) | glimlag | [χlimlaχ] |

to speak (vi, vt)	praat	[prãt]
to steal (money, etc.)	steel	[steel]
to stop (for pause, etc.)	stilhou	[stilhæʊ]
to stop (please ~ calling me)	ophou	[ophæʊ]
to study (vt)	studeer	[studeer]
to swim (vi)	swem	[swem]
to take (vt)	vat	[fat]
to think (vi, vt)	dink	[dink]
to threaten (vt)	dreig	[dræjχ]
to touch (with hands)	aanraak	[ãnrãk]
to translate (vt)	vertaal	[fertãl]
to trust (vt)	vertrou	[fertræʊ]
to try (attempt)	probeer	[probeer]
to turn (e.g., ~ left)	draai	[drãi]
to underestimate (vt)	onderskat	[ondərskat]
to understand (vt)	verstaan	[ferstãn]
to unite (vt)	verenig	[ferenəχ]
to wait (vt)	wag	[vaχ]
to want (wish, desire)	wil	[vil]
to warn (vt)	waarsku	[vãrsku]
to work (vi)	werk	[verk]
to write (vt)	skryf	[skrajf]
to write down	opskryf	[opskrajf]

12. Colours

colour	kleur	[kløer]
shade (tint)	skakering	[skakeriŋ]
hue	tint	[tint]
rainbow	reënboog	[reɛn·boəχ]
white (adj)	wit	[vit]
black (adj)	swart	[swart]
grey (adj)	grys	[χrajs]
green (adj)	groen	[χrun]
yellow (adj)	geel	[χeəl]
red (adj)	rooi	[roj]
blue (adj)	blou	[blæʊ]
light blue (adj)	ligblou	[liχ·blæʊ]
pink (adj)	pienk	[pink]
orange (adj)	oranje	[oranje]
violet (adj)	pers	[pers]
brown (adj)	bruin	[brœin]
golden (adj)	goue	[χæʊə]
silvery (adj)	silweragtig	[silweraχtəχ]
beige (adj)	beige	[bɛːiʒ]
cream (adj)	roomkleurig	[roəm·kløərəχ]

turquoise (adj)	**turkoois**	[turkojs]
cherry red (adj)	**kersierooi**	[kersi·roj]
lilac (adj)	**lila**	[lila]
crimson (adj)	**karmosyn**	[karmosajn]
light (adj)	**lig**	[liχ]
dark (adj)	**donker**	[donkər]
bright, vivid (adj)	**helder**	[hɛldər]
coloured (pencils)	**kleurig**	[kløərəχ]
colour (e.g. ~ film)	**kleur**	[kløər]
black-and-white (adj)	**swart-wit**	[swart-wit]
plain (one-coloured)	**effe**	[ɛffə]
multicoloured (adj)	**veelkleurig**	[feəlkløərəχ]

13. Questions

Who?	**Wie?**	[vi?]
What?	**Wat?**	[vat?]
Where? (at, in)	**Waar?**	[vãr?]
Where (to)?	**Waarheen?**	[vãrheən?]
From where?	**Waarvandaan?**	[vãrfandãn?]
When?	**Wanneer?**	[vanneər?]
Why? (What for?)	**Hoekom?**	[hukom?]
Why? (~ are you crying?)	**Hoekom?**	[hukom?]
What for?	**Vir wat?**	[fir vat?]
How? (in what way)	**Hoe?**	[hu?]
What? (What kind of ...?)	**Watter?**	[vattər?]
Which?	**Watter een?**	[vattər eən?]
To whom?	**Vir wie?**	[fir vi?]
About whom?	**Oor wie?**	[oər vi?]
About what?	**Oor wat?**	[oər vat?]
With whom?	**Met wie?**	[met vi?]
How many? How much?	**Hoeveel?**	[hufeəl?]

14. Function words. Adverbs. Part 1

Where? (at, in)	**Waar?**	[vãr?]
here (adv)	**hier**	[hir]
there (adv)	**daar**	[dãr]
somewhere (to be)	**êrens**	[ærɛŋs]
nowhere (not in any place)	**nêrens**	[nærɛŋs]
by (near, beside)	**by**	[baj]
by the window	**by**	[baj]
Where (to)?	**Waarheen?**	[vãrheən?]
here (e.g. come ~!)	**hier**	[hir]
there (e.g. to go ~)	**soontoe**	[soentu]

from here (adv)	hiervandaan	[hirfandãn]
from there (adv)	daarvandaan	[dãrfandãn]
close (adv)	naby	[nabaj]
far (adv)	ver	[fer]
near (e.g. ~ Paris)	naby	[nabaj]
nearby (adv)	naby	[nabaj]
not far (adv)	nie ver nie	[ni fər ni]
left (adj)	linker-	[linkər-]
on the left	op linkerhand	[op linkərhant]
to the left	na links	[na links]
right (adj)	regter	[reχtər]
on the right	op regterhand	[op reχtərhant]
to the right	na regs	[na reχs]
in front (adv)	voor	[foər]
front (as adj)	voorste	[foərstə]
ahead (the kids ran ~)	vooruit	[foərœit]
behind (adv)	agter	[aχtər]
from behind	van agter	[fan aχtər]
back (towards the rear)	agtertoe	[aχtərtu]
middle	middel	[middəl]
in the middle	in die middel	[in di middəl]
at the side	op die sykant	[op di sajkant]
everywhere (adv)	orals	[orals]
around (in all directions)	orals rond	[orals ront]
from inside	van binne	[fan binnə]
somewhere (to go)	êrens	[ærɛŋs]
straight (directly)	reguit	[reχœit]
back (e.g. come ~)	terug	[teruχ]
from anywhere	êrens vandaan	[ærɛŋs fandãn]
from somewhere	êrens vandaan	[ærɛŋs fandãn]
firstly (adv)	in die eerste plek	[in di eərstə plek]
secondly (adv)	in die tweede plek	[in di tweədə plek]
thirdly (adv)	in die derde plek	[in di derdə plek]
suddenly (adv)	skielik	[skilik]
at first (in the beginning)	aan die begin	[ãn di beχin]
for the first time	vir die eerste keer	[fir di eərstə keər]
long before ...	lank voordat ...	[lank foərdat ...]
anew (over again)	opnuut	[opnɪt]
for good (adv)	vir goed	[fir χut]
never (adv)	nooit	[nojt]
again (adv)	weer	[veər]
now (at present)	nou	[næʊ]
often (adv)	dikwels	[dikwɛls]

then (adv)	**toe**	[tu]
urgently (quickly)	**dringend**	[driŋən]
usually (adv)	**gewoonlik**	[χevoənlik]
by the way, …	**terloops, …**	[terloəps], […]
possibly	**moontlik**	[moentlik]
probably (adv)	**waarskynlik**	[vārskajnlik]
maybe (adv)	**dalk**	[dalk]
besides …	**trouens …**	[træʊɛŋs …]
that's why …	**dis hoekom …**	[dis hukom …]
in spite of …	**ondanks …**	[ondanks …]
thanks to …	**danksy …**	[danksaj …]
what (pron.)	**wat**	[vat]
that (conj.)	**dat**	[dat]
something	**iets**	[its]
anything (something)	**iets**	[its]
nothing	**niks**	[niks]
who (pron.)	**wie**	[vi]
someone	**iemand**	[imant]
somebody	**iemand**	[imant]
nobody	**niemand**	[nimant]
nowhere (a voyage to ~)	**nêrens**	[nærɛŋs]
nobody's	**niemand se**	[nimant sə]
somebody's	**iemand se**	[imant sə]
so (I'm ~ glad)	**so**	[so]
also (as well)	**ook**	[oək]
too (as well)	**ook**	[oək]

15. Function words. Adverbs. Part 2

Why?	**Waarom?**	[vārom?]
because …	**omdat …**	[omdat …]
and	**en**	[ɛn]
or	**of**	[of]
but	**maar**	[mār]
for (e.g. ~ me)	**vir**	[fir]
too (excessively)	**te**	[te]
only (exclusively)	**net**	[net]
exactly (adv)	**presies**	[presis]
about (more or less)	**ongeveer**	[onχəfeər]
approximately (adv)	**ongeveer**	[onχəfeər]
approximate (adj)	**geraamde**	[χerāmdə]
almost (adv)	**amper**	[ampər]
the rest	**die res**	[di res]
the other (second)	**die ander**	[di andər]
other (different)	**ander**	[andər]

each (adj)	elke	[ɛlkə]
any (no matter which)	enige	[ɛniχə]
many (adj)	baie	[baje]
much (adv)	baie	[baje]
many people	baie mense	[baje mɛŋsə]
all (everyone)	almal	[almal]

in return for ...	in ruil vir ...	[in rœil fir ...]
in exchange (adv)	as vergoeding	[as ferχudiŋ]
by hand (made)	met die hand	[met di hant]
hardly (negative opinion)	skaars	[skārs]

probably (adv)	waarskynlik	[vārskajnlik]
on purpose (intentionally)	opsetlik	[opsetlik]
by accident (adv)	toevallig	[tufalləχ]

very (adv)	baie	[baje]
for example (adv)	byvoorbeeld	[bajfoərbeəlt]
between	tussen	[tussən]
among	tussen	[tussən]
so much (such a lot)	so baie	[so baje]
especially (adv)	veral	[feral]

Basic concepts. Part 2

16. Opposites

rich (adj)	ryk	[rajk]
poor (adj)	arm	[arm]
ill, sick (adj)	siek	[sik]
well (not sick)	gesond	[χesont]
big (adj)	groot	[χroət]
small (adj)	klein	[klæjn]
quickly (adv)	vinnig	[finnəχ]
slowly (adv)	stadig	[stadəχ]
fast (adj)	vinnig	[finnəχ]
slow (adj)	stadig	[stadəχ]
glad (adj)	bly	[blaj]
sad (adj)	droewig	[druvəχ]
together (adv)	saam	[sãm]
separately (adv)	afsonderlik	[afsondərlik]
aloud (to read)	hardop	[hardop]
silently (to oneself)	stil	[stil]
tall (adj)	groot	[χroət]
low (adj)	laag	[lãχ]
deep (adj)	diep	[dip]
shallow (adj)	vlak	[flak]
yes	ja	[ja]
no	nee	[neə]
distant (in space)	ver	[fer]
nearby (adj)	naby	[nabaj]
far (adv)	ver	[fer]
nearby (adv)	naby	[nabaj]
long (adj)	lang	[laŋ]
short (adj)	kort	[kort]
good (kindhearted)	vriendelik	[frindəlik]
evil (adj)	boos	[boəs]

| married (adj) | getroud | [χetræʊt] |
| single (adj) | ongetroud | [onχətræʊt] |

| to forbid (vt) | verbied | [ferbit] |
| to permit (vt) | toestaan | [tustān] |

| end | einde | [æjndə] |
| beginning | begin | [beχin] |

| left (adj) | linker- | [linkər-] |
| right (adj) | regter | [reχtər] |

| first (adj) | eerste | [eərstə] |
| last (adj) | laaste | [lāstə] |

| crime | misdaad | [misdāt] |
| punishment | straf | [straf] |

| to order (vt) | beveel | [befeəl] |
| to obey (vi, vt) | gehoorsaam | [χehoərsām] |

| straight (adj) | reguit | [reχœit] |
| curved (adj) | krom | [krom] |

| paradise | paradys | [paradajs] |
| hell | hel | [həl] |

| to be born | gebore word | [χeborə vort] |
| to die (vi) | doodgaan | [doədχān] |

| strong (adj) | sterk | [sterk] |
| weak (adj) | swak | [swak] |

| old (adj) | oud | [æʊt] |
| young (adj) | jong | [joŋ] |

| old (adj) | ou | [æʊ] |
| new (adj) | nuwe | [nuvə] |

| hard (adj) | hard | [hart] |
| soft (adj) | sag | [saχ] |

| warm (tepid) | warm | [varm] |
| cold (adj) | koud | [kæʊt] |

| fat (adj) | vet | [fet] |
| thin (adj) | dun | [dun] |

| narrow (adj) | smal | [smal] |
| wide (adj) | wyd | [vajt] |

| good (adj) | goed | [χut] |
| bad (adj) | sleg | [sleχ] |

| brave (adj) | dapper | [dappər] |
| cowardly (adj) | lafhartig | [lafhartəχ] |

17. Weekdays

Monday	**Maandag**	[māndaχ]
Tuesday	**Dinsdag**	[dinsdaχ]
Wednesday	**Woensdag**	[voɛŋsdaχ]
Thursday	**Donderdag**	[dondərdaχ]
Friday	**Vrydag**	[frajdaχ]
Saturday	**Saterdag**	[satərdaχ]
Sunday	**Sondag**	[sondaχ]
today (adv)	**vandag**	[fandaχ]
tomorrow (adv)	**môre**	[mɔrə]
the day after tomorrow	**oormôre**	[oərmɔrə]
yesterday (adv)	**gister**	[χistər]
the day before yesterday	**eergister**	[eərχistər]
day	**dag**	[daχ]
working day	**werksdag**	[verks·daχ]
public holiday	**openbare vakansiedag**	[openbarə fakaŋsi·daχ]
day off	**verlofdag**	[ferlofdaχ]
weekend	**naweek**	[naveək]
all day long	**die hele dag**	[di helə daχ]
the next day (adv)	**die volgende dag**	[di folχendə daχ]
two days ago	**twee dae gelede**	[tweə daə χeledə]
the day before	**die dag voor**	[di daχ foər]
daily (adj)	**daeliks**	[daəliks]
every day (adv)	**elke dag**	[ɛlkə daχ]
week	**week**	[veək]
last week (adv)	**laas week**	[lās veək]
next week (adv)	**volgende week**	[folχendə veək]
weekly (adj)	**weekliks**	[veəkliks]
every week (adv)	**weekliks**	[veəkliks]
every Tuesday	**elke Dinsdag**	[ɛlkə dinsdaχ]

18. Hours. Day and night

morning	**oggend**	[oχent]
in the morning	**soggens**	[soχɛŋs]
noon, midday	**middag**	[middaχ]
in the afternoon	**in die namiddag**	[in di namiddaχ]
evening	**aand**	[ānt]
in the evening	**saans**	[sāŋs]
night	**nag**	[naχ]
at night	**snags**	[snaχs]
midnight	**middernag**	[middərnaχ]
second	**sekonde**	[sekondə]
minute	**minuut**	[minɪt]
hour	**uur**	[ɪr]
half an hour	**n halfuur**	[n halfɪr]

| fifteen minutes | vyftien minute | [fajftin minutə] |
| 24 hours | 24 ure | [fir-en-twintəχ urə] |

sunrise	sonop	[son·op]
dawn	daeraad	[daerãt]
early morning	elke oggend	[ɛlkə oχent]
sunset	sononder	[son·ondər]

early in the morning	vroegdag	[fruχdaχ]
this morning	vanmôre	[fanmɔrə]
tomorrow morning	môreoggend	[mɔrə·oχent]

this afternoon	vanmiddag	[fanmiddaχ]
in the afternoon	in die namiddag	[in di namiddaχ]
tomorrow afternoon	môremiddag	[mɔrə·middaχ]

| tonight (this evening) | vanaand | [fanãnt] |
| tomorrow night | môreaand | [mɔrə·ãnt] |

at 3 o'clock sharp	klokslag 3 uur	[klokslaχ dri ɪr]
about 4 o'clock	omstreeks 4 uur	[omstreeks fir ɪr]
by 12 o'clock	teen 12 uur	[teən twalf ɪr]

| in 20 minutes | oor twintig minute | [oər twintəχ minutə] |
| on time (adv) | betyds | [betajds] |

a quarter to ...	kwart voor ...	[kwart foər ...]
every 15 minutes	elke 15 minute	[ɛlkə fajftin minutə]
round the clock	24 uur per dag	[fir-en-twintəχ pər daχ]

19. Months. Seasons

January	Januarie	[januari]
February	Februarie	[februari]
March	Maart	[mãrt]
April	April	[april]
May	Mei	[mæj]
June	Junie	[juni]

July	Julie	[juli]
August	Augustus	[ɔuχustus]
September	September	[septembər]
October	Oktober	[oktobər]
November	November	[nofembər]
December	Desember	[desembər]

spring	lente	[lentə]
in spring	in die lente	[in di lentə]
spring (as adj)	lente-	[lente-]

summer	somer	[somər]
in summer	in die somer	[in di somər]
summer (as adj)	somerse	[somersə]
autumn	herfs	[herfs]

| in autumn | in die herfs | [in di herfs] |
| autumn (as adj) | herfsagtige | [herfsaχtiχə] |

winter	winter	[vintər]
in winter	in die winter	[in di vintər]
winter (as adj)	winter-	[vintər-]

month	maand	[mānt]
this month	hierdie maand	[hirdi mānt]
next month	volgende maand	[folχendə mānt]
last month	laasmaand	[lāsmānt]

| in 2 months (2 months later) | oor twe maande | [oər twə māndə] |
| the whole month | die hele maand | [di helə mānt] |

monthly (~ magazine)	maandeliks	[māndəliks]
monthly (adv)	maandeliks	[māndəliks]
every month	elke maand	[ɛlkə mānt]

year	jaar	[jār]
this year	hierdie jaar	[hirdi jār]
next year	volgende jaar	[folχendə jār]
last year	laasjaar	[lāʃār]

| in two years | binne twee jaar | [binnə tweə jār] |
| the whole year | die hele jaar | [di helə jār] |

every year	elke jaar	[ɛlkə jār]
annual (adj)	jaarliks	[jārliks]
annually (adv)	jaarliks	[jārliks]
4 times a year	4 keer per jaar	[fir keər pər jār]

date (e.g. today's ~)	datum	[datum]
date (e.g. ~ of birth)	datum	[datum]
calendar	kalender	[kalendər]

six months	ses maande	[ses māndə]
season (summer, etc.)	seisoen	[sæjsun]
century	eeu	[iʊ]

20. Time. Miscellaneous

time	tyd	[tajt]
moment	moment	[moment]
instant (n)	oomblik	[oəmblik]
instant (adj)	oombliklik	[oəmbliklik]
lapse (of time)	tydbestek	[tajdbestək]
life	lewe	[levə]
eternity	ewigheid	[ɛviχæjt]

epoch	tydperk	[tajtperk]
era	tydperk	[tajtperk]
cycle	siklus	[siklus]
period	periode	[periodə]

term (short-~)	termyn	[termajn]
the future	die toekoms	[di tukoms]
future (as adj)	toekomstig	[tukomstəχ]
next time	die volgende keer	[di folχendə keər]
the past	die verlede	[di ferledə]
past (recent)	laas-	[lãs-]
last time	die vorige keer	[di foriχə keər]
later (adv)	later	[latər]
after (prep.)	na	[na]
nowadays (adv)	deesdae	[deəsdaə]
now (at this moment)	nou	[næʊ]
immediately (adv)	onmiddellik	[onmiddɛllik]
soon (adv)	gou	[χæʊ]
in advance (beforehand)	by voorbaat	[baj foərbãt]
a long time ago	lank gelede	[lank χeledə]
recently (adv)	onlangs	[onlaŋs]
destiny	noodlot	[noədlot]
recollections	herinneringe	[herinneriŋə]
archives	argiewe	[arχivə]
during ...	gedurende ...	[χedurendə ...]
long, a long time (adv)	lank	[lank]
not long (adv)	nie lank nie	[ni lank ni]
early (in the morning)	vroeg	[fruχ]
late (not early)	laat	[lãt]
forever (for good)	vir altyd	[fir altajt]
to start (begin)	begin	[beχin]
to postpone (vt)	uitstel	[œitstəl]
at the same time	tegelykertyd	[teχelajkertajt]
permanently (adv)	permanent	[permanent]
constant (noise, pain)	voortdurend	[foərtdurent]
temporary (adj)	tydelik	[tajdelik]
sometimes (adv)	soms	[soms]
rarely (adv)	selde	[sɛldə]
often (adv)	dikwels	[dikwɛls]

21. Lines and shapes

square	vierkant	[firkant]
square (as adj)	vierkantig	[firkantəχ]
circle	sirkel	[sirkəl]
round (adj)	rond	[ront]
triangle	driehoek	[drihuk]
triangular (adj)	driehoekig	[drihukəχ]
oval	ovaal	[ofãl]
oval (as adj)	ovaal	[ofãl]
rectangle	reghoek	[reχhuk]
rectangular (adj)	reghoekig	[reχhukəχ]

pyramid	piramide	[piramidə]
rhombus	ruit	[rœit]
trapezium	trapesoïed	[trapesoïət]
cube	kubus	[kubus]
prism	prisma	[prisma]

circumference	omtrek	[omtrək]
sphere	sfeer	[sfeər]
ball (solid sphere)	bal	[bal]
diameter	diameter	[diametər]
radius	straal	[strāl]
perimeter (circle's ~)	omtrek	[omtrək]
centre	sentrum	[sentrum]

horizontal (adj)	horisontaal	[horisontāl]
vertical (adj)	vertikaal	[fertikāl]
parallel (n)	parallel	[paralləl]
parallel (as adj)	parallel	[paralləl]

line	lyn	[lajn]
stroke	haal	[hāl]
straight line	regte lyn	[reχtə lajn]
curve (curved line)	krom	[krom]
thin (line, etc.)	dun	[dun]
contour (outline)	omtrek	[omtrək]

intersection	snypunt	[snaj·punt]
right angle	regte hoek	[reχtə huk]
segment	segment	[seχment]
sector (circular ~)	sektor	[sektor]
side (of a triangle)	sy	[saj]
angle	hoek	[huk]

22. Units of measurement

weight	gewig	[χevəχ]
length	lengte	[leŋtə]
width	breedte	[breedtə]
height	hoogte	[hoəχtə]
depth	diepte	[diptə]
volume	volume	[folumə]
area	area	[area]

gram	gram	[χram]
milligram	milligram	[milliχram]
kilogram	kilogram	[kiloχram]
ton	ton	[ton]
pound	pond	[pont]
ounce	ons	[ɔŋs]

metre	meter	[metər]
millimetre	millimeter	[millimetər]
centimetre	sentimeter	[sentimetər]
kilometre	kilometer	[kilometər]

mile	myl	[majl]
inch	duim	[dœim]
foot	voet	[fut]
yard	jaart	[jãrt]

| square metre | vierkante meter | [firkantə metər] |
| hectare | hektaar | [hektãr] |

litre	liter	[litər]
degree	graad	[xrãt]
volt	volt	[folt]
ampere	ampère	[ampε:r]
horsepower	perdekrag	[perdə·kraχ]

quantity	hoeveelheid	[hufeəlhæjt]
half	helfte	[hɛlftə]
dozen	dosyn	[dosajn]
piece (item)	stuk	[stuk]

| size | grootte | [xroəttə] |
| scale (map ~) | skaal | [skãl] |

minimal (adj)	minimaal	[minimãl]
the smallest (adj)	die kleinste	[di klæjnstə]
medium (adj)	medium	[medium]
maximal (adj)	maksimaal	[maksimãl]
the largest (adj)	die grootste	[di χroətstə]

23. Containers

canning jar (glass ~)	glaspot	[χlas·pot]
tin, can	blikkie	[blikki]
bucket	emmer	[ɛmmər]
barrel	drom	[drom]

wash basin (e.g., plastic ~)	wasbak	[vas·bak]
tank (100L water ~)	tenk	[tɛnk]
hip flask	heupfles	[høəp·fles]
jerrycan	petrolblik	[petrol·blik]
tank (e.g., tank car)	tenk	[tɛnk]

mug	beker	[bekər]
cup (of coffee, etc.)	koppie	[koppi]
saucer	piering	[pirin]
glass (tumbler)	glas	[χlas]
wine glass	wynglas	[vajn·χlas]
stock pot (soup pot)	soppot	[sop·pot]

| bottle (~ of wine) | bottel | [bottəl] |
| neck (of the bottle, etc.) | nek | [nek] |

carafe (decanter)	kraffie	[kraffi]
pitcher	kruik	[krœik]
vessel (container)	houer	[hæʊər]

| pot (crock, stoneware ~) | pot | [pot] |
| vase | vaas | [fãs] |

flacon, bottle (perfume ~)	bottel	[bottəl]
vial, small bottle	botteltjie	[bottɛlki]
tube (of toothpaste)	buisie	[bœisi]

sack (bag)	sak	[sak]
bag (paper ~, plastic ~)	sak	[sak]
packet (of cigarettes, etc.)	pakkie	[pakki]

box (e.g. shoebox)	kartondoos	[karton·does]
crate	krat	[krat]
basket	mandjie	[mandʒi]

24. Materials

material	boustof	[bæʊstof]
wood (n)	hout	[hæʊt]
wood-, wooden (adj)	hout-	[hæʊt-]

| glass (n) | glas | [χlas] |
| glass (as adj) | glas- | [χlas-] |

| stone (n) | klip | [klip] |
| stone (as adj) | klip- | [klip-] |

| plastic (n) | plastiek | [plastik] |
| plastic (as adj) | plastiek- | [plastik-] |

| rubber (n) | rubber | [rubbər] |
| rubber (as adj) | rubber- | [rubbər-] |

| cloth, fabric (n) | materiaal | [materiãl] |
| fabric (as adj) | materiaal- | [materiãl-] |

| paper (n) | papier | [papir] |
| paper (as adj) | papier- | [papir-] |

| cardboard (n) | karton | [karton] |
| cardboard (as adj) | karton- | [karton-] |

| polyethylene | politeen | [politeən] |
| cellophane | sellofaan | [sɛllofãn] |

| linoleum | linoleum | [linoløəm] |
| plywood | laaghout | [lãχhæʊt] |

porcelain (n)	porselein	[porselæjn]
porcelain (as adj)	porselein-	[porselæjn-]
clay (n)	klei	[klæj]
clay (as adj)	klei-	[klæj-]
ceramic (n)	keramiek	[keramik]
ceramic (as adj)	keramiek-	[keramik-]

25. Metals

metal (n)	**metaal**	[metãl]
metal (as adj)	**metaal-**	[metãl-]
alloy (n)	**allooi**	[alloj]
gold (n)	**goud**	[χæʊt]
gold, golden (adj)	**goue**	[χæʊə]
silver (n)	**silwer**	[silwər]
silver (as adj)	**silwer-**	[silwər-]
iron (n)	**yster**	[ajstər]
iron-, made of iron (adj)	**yster-**	[ajstər-]
steel (n)	**staal**	[stãl]
steel (as adj)	**staal-**	[stãl-]
copper (n)	**koper**	[kopər]
copper (as adj)	**koper-**	[kopər-]
aluminium (n)	**aluminium**	[aluminium]
aluminium (as adj)	**aluminium-**	[aluminium-]
bronze (n)	**brons**	[brɔŋs]
bronze (as adj)	**brons-**	[brɔŋs-]
brass	**geelkoper**	[χeəl·kopər]
nickel	**nikkel**	[nikkəl]
platinum	**platinum**	[platinum]
mercury	**kwik**	[kwik]
tin	**tin**	[tin]
lead	**lood**	[loət]
zinc	**sink**	[sink]

HUMAN BEING

Human being. The body

human being	**mens**	[mɛŋs]
man (adult male)	**man**	[man]
woman	**vrou**	[fræʊ]
child	**kind**	[kint]
girl	**meisie**	[mæjsi]
boy	**seun**	[søən]
teenager	**tiener**	[tinər]
old man	**ou man**	[æʊ man]
old woman	**ou vrou**	[æʊ fræʊ]

organism (body)	**organisme**	[orχanismə]
heart	**hart**	[hart]
blood	**bloed**	[blut]
artery	**slagaar**	[slaχãr]
vein	**aar**	[ãr]
brain	**brein**	[bræjn]
nerve	**senuwee**	[senuveə]
nerves	**senuwees**	[senuveəs]
vertebra	**rugwerwels**	[ruχ·werwɛls]
spine (backbone)	**ruggraat**	[ruχ·χrãt]
stomach (organ)	**maag**	[mãχ]
intestines, bowels	**ingewande**	[inχəwandə]
intestine (e.g. large ~)	**derm**	[derm]
liver	**lewer**	[levər]
kidney	**nier**	[nir]
bone	**been**	[beən]
skeleton	**geraamte**	[χerãmtə]
rib	**rib**	[rip]
skull	**skedel**	[skedəl]
muscle	**spier**	[spir]
biceps	**biseps**	[biseps]
triceps	**triseps**	[triseps]
tendon	**sening**	[seniŋ]
joint	**gewrig**	[χevrəχ]

lungs	longe	[loŋə]
genitals	geslagsorgane	[χeslaχs·orχanə]
skin	vel	[fəl]

28. Head

head	kop	[kop]
face	gesig	[χesəχ]
nose	neus	[nøəs]
mouth	mond	[mont]

eye	oog	[oəχ]
eyes	oë	[oɛ]
pupil	pupil	[pupil]
eyebrow	wenkbrou	[vɛnk·bræʊ]
eyelash	ooghaar	[oəχ·hãr]
eyelid	ooglid	[oəχ·lit]

tongue	tong	[toŋ]
tooth	tand	[tant]
lips	lippe	[lippə]
cheekbones	wangbene	[vaŋ·benə]
gum	tandvleis	[tand·flæjs]
palate	verhemelte	[fer·hemɛltə]

nostrils	neusgate	[nøəsχatə]
chin	ken	[ken]
jaw	kakebeen	[kakebeən]
cheek	wang	[vaŋ]

forehead	voorhoof	[foərhoəf]
temple	slaap	[slãp]
ear	oor	[oər]
back of the head	agterkop	[aχtərkop]
neck	nek	[nek]
throat	keel	[keəl]

hair	haar	[hãr]
hairstyle	kapsel	[kapsəl]
haircut	haarstyl	[hãrstajl]
wig	pruik	[prœik]

moustache	snor	[snor]
beard	baard	[bãrt]
to have (a beard, etc.)	dra	[dra]
plait	vlegsel	[fleχsəl]
sideboards	bakkebaarde	[bakkəbãrdə]

red-haired (adj)	rooiharig	[roj·harəχ]
grey (hair)	grys	[χrajs]
bald (adj)	kaal	[kãl]
bald patch	kaal plek	[kãl plek]
ponytail	poniestert	[poni·stert]
fringe	gordyntjiekapsel	[χordajnki·kapsəl]

29. Human body

hand	**hand**	[hant]
arm	**arm**	[arm]
finger	**vinger**	[fiŋər]
toe	**toon**	[toən]
thumb	**duim**	[dœim]
little finger	**pinkie**	[pinki]
nail	**nael**	[naəl]
fist	**vuis**	[fœis]
palm	**palm**	[palm]
wrist	**pols**	[pols]
forearm	**voorarm**	[foərarm]
elbow	**elmboog**	[ɛlmboəχ]
shoulder	**skouer**	[skæʊər]
leg	**been**	[beən]
foot	**voet**	[fut]
knee	**knie**	[kni]
calf	**kuit**	[kœit]
hip	**heup**	[høəp]
heel	**hakskeen**	[hak·skeən]
body	**liggaam**	[liχχãm]
stomach	**maag**	[mãχ]
chest	**bors**	[bors]
breast	**bors**	[bors]
flank	**sy**	[saj]
back	**rug**	[ruχ]
lower back	**lae rug**	[laə ruχ]
waist	**middel**	[middəl]
navel (belly button)	**naeltjie**	[naɛlki]
buttocks	**boude**	[bæʊdə]
bottom	**sitvlak**	[sitflak]
beauty spot	**moesie**	[musi]
birthmark (café au lait spot)	**moedervlek**	[mudər·flek]
tattoo	**tatoe**	[tatu]
scar	**litteken**	[littekən]

Clothing & Accessories

30. Outerwear. Coats

clothes	klere	[klerə]
outerwear	oorklere	[oərklerə]
winter clothing	winterklere	[vintər·klerə]
coat (overcoat)	jas	[jas]
fur coat	pelsjas	[pelʃas]
fur jacket	kort pelsjas	[kort pelʃas]
down coat	donsjas	[donʃas]
jacket (e.g. leather ~)	baadjie	[bādʒi]
raincoat (trenchcoat, etc.)	reënjas	[reenjas]
waterproof (adj)	waterdig	[vatərdəχ]

31. Men's & women's clothing

shirt (button shirt)	hemp	[hemp]
trousers	broek	[bruk]
jeans	denimbroek	[denim·bruk]
suit jacket	baadjie	[bādʒi]
suit	pak	[pak]
dress (frock)	rok	[rok]
skirt	romp	[romp]
blouse	bloes	[blus]
knitted jacket (cardigan, etc.)	gebreide baadjie	[χebræjdə bādʒi]
jacket (of a woman's suit)	baadjie	[bādʒi]
T-shirt	T-hemp	[te-hemp]
shorts (short trousers)	kortbroek	[kort·bruk]
tracksuit	sweetpak	[sweet·pak]
bathrobe	badjas	[batjas]
pyjamas	pajama	[pajama]
jumper (sweater)	trui	[trœi]
pullover	trui	[trœi]
waistcoat	onderbaadjie	[ondər·bādʒi]
tailcoat	swaelstertbaadjie	[swaɛlstert·bādʒi]
dinner suit	aandpak	[āntpak]
uniform	uniform	[uniform]
workwear	werksklere	[verks·klerə]
boiler suit	oorpak	[oərpak]
coat (e.g. doctor's smock)	jas	[jas]

32. Clothing. Underwear

underwear	**onderklere**	[ondərklerə]
pants	**onderbroek**	[ondərbruk]
panties	**onderbroek**	[ondərbruk]
vest (singlet)	**frokkie**	[frokki]
socks	**sokkies**	[sokkis]
nightdress	**nagrok**	[naχrok]
bra	**bra**	[bra]
knee highs (knee-high socks)	**kniekouse**	[kni·kæʊsə]
tights	**kousbroek**	[kæʊsbruk]
stockings (hold ups)	**kouse**	[kæʊsə]
swimsuit, bikini	**baaikostuum**	[bāj·kostɪm]

33. Headwear

hat	**hoed**	[hut]
trilby hat	**hoed**	[hut]
baseball cap	**bofbalpet**	[bofbal·pet]
flatcap	**pet**	[pet]
beret	**mus**	[mus]
hood	**kap**	[kap]
panama hat	**panamahoed**	[panama·hut]
knit cap (knitted hat)	**gebreide mus**	[χebræjdə mus]
headscarf	**kopdoek**	[kopduk]
women's hat	**dameshoed**	[dames·hut]
hard hat	**veiligheidshelm**	[fæjliχæjts·hɛlm]
forage cap	**mus**	[mus]
helmet	**helmet**	[hɛlmet]
bowler	**bolhoed**	[bolhut]
top hat	**hoëhoed**	[hoɛhut]

34. Footwear

footwear	**skoeisel**	[skuisəl]
shoes (men's shoes)	**mansskoene**	[maŋs·skunə]
shoes (women's shoes)	**damesskoene**	[dames·skunə]
boots (e.g., cowboy ~)	**laarse**	[lārsə]
carpet slippers	**pantoffels**	[pantoffəls]
trainers	**tennisskoene**	[tɛnnis·skunə]
trainers	**tekkies**	[tɛkkis]
sandals	**sandale**	[sandalə]
cobbler (shoe repairer)	**skoenmaker**	[skun·makər]
heel	**hak**	[hak]

pair (of shoes)	**paar**	[pār]
lace (shoelace)	**skoenveter**	[skun·fetər]
to lace up (vt)	**ryg**	[rajχ]
shoehorn	**skoenlepel**	[skun·lepəl]
shoe polish	**skoenpolitoer**	[skun·politur]

35. Textile. Fabrics

cotton (n)	**katoen**	[katun]
cotton (as adj)	**katoen-**	[katun-]
flax (n)	**vlas**	[flas]
flax (as adj)	**vlas-**	[flas-]

silk (n)	**sy**	[saj]
silk (as adj)	**sy-**	[saj-]
wool (n)	**wol**	[vol]
wool (as adj)	**wol-**	[vol-]

velvet	**fluweel**	[fluveəl]
suede	**suède**	[suɛdə]
corduroy	**ferweel**	[ferweəl]

nylon (n)	**nylon**	[najlon]
nylon (as adj)	**nylon-**	[najlon-]
polyester (n)	**poliëster**	[poliɛstər]
polyester (as adj)	**poliëster-**	[poliɛstər-]

leather (n)	**leer**	[leər]
leather (as adj)	**leer-**	[leər-]
fur (n)	**bont**	[bont]
fur (e.g. ~ coat)	**bont-**	[bont-]

36. Personal accessories

gloves	**handskoene**	[handskunə]
mittens	**duimhandskoene**	[dœim·handskunə]
scarf (muffler)	**serp**	[serp]

glasses	**bril**	[bril]
frame (eyeglass ~)	**raam**	[rām]
umbrella	**sambreel**	[sambreəl]
walking stick	**wandelstok**	[vandəl·stok]
hairbrush	**haarborsel**	[hār·borsəl]
fan	**waaier**	[vājer]

tie (necktie)	**das**	[das]
bow tie	**strikkie**	[strikki]
braces	**kruisbande**	[krœis·bandə]
handkerchief	**sakdoek**	[sakduk]

| comb | **kam** | [kam] |
| hair slide | **haarspeld** | [hārs·pɛlt] |

| hairpin | haarpen | [hār·pen] |
| buckle | gespe | [χespə] |

| belt | belt | [bɛlt] |
| shoulder strap | skouerband | [skæʋer·bant] |

bag (handbag)	handsak	[hand·sak]
handbag	beursie	[bøərsi]
rucksack	rugsak	[ruχsak]

37. Clothing. Miscellaneous

fashion	mode	[modə]
in vogue (adj)	in die mode	[in di modə]
fashion designer	modeontwerper	[modə·ontwerpər]

collar	kraag	[krāχ]
pocket	sak	[sak]
pocket (as adj)	sak-	[sak-]
sleeve	mou	[mæʋ]
hanging loop	lussie	[lussi]
flies (on trousers)	gulp	[χulp]

zip (fastener)	ritssluiter	[rits·slœitər]
fastener	vasmaker	[fasmakər]
button	knoop	[knoəp]
buttonhole	knoopsgat	[knoəps·χat]
to come off (ab. button)	loskom	[loskom]

to sew (vi, vt)	naai	[nāi]
to embroider (vi, vt)	borduur	[bordɪr]
embroidery	borduurwerk	[bordɪr·werk]
sewing needle	naald	[nālt]
thread	garing	[χariŋ]
seam	soom	[soəm]

to get dirty (vi)	vuil word	[fœil vort]
stain (mark, spot)	vlek	[flek]
to crease, to crumple	kreukel	[krøəkəl]
to tear, to rip (vt)	skeur	[skøər]
clothes moth	mot	[mot]

38. Personal care. Cosmetics

toothpaste	tandepasta	[tandə·pasta]
toothbrush	tandeborsel	[tandə·borsəl]
to clean one's teeth	tande borsel	[tandə borsəl]

razor	skeermes	[skeər·mes]
shaving cream	skeerroom	[skeər·roəm]
to shave (vi)	skeer	[skeər]
soap	seep	[seəp]

shampoo	**sjampoe**	[ʃampu]
scissors	**skêr**	[skær]
nail file	**naelvyl**	[naɛl·fajl]
nail clippers	**naelknipper**	[naɛl·knippər]
tweezers	**haartangetjie**	[hãrtaŋəki]
cosmetics	**kosmetika**	[kosmetika]
face mask	**gesigmasker**	[xesiχ·maskər]
manicure	**manikuur**	[manikɪr]
to have a manicure	**laat manikuur**	[lãt manikɪr]
pedicure	**voetbehandeling**	[fut·behandeliŋ]
make-up bag	**kosmetika tassie**	[kosmetika tassi]
face powder	**gesigpoeier**	[xesiχ·pujer]
powder compact	**poeierdosie**	[pujer·dosi]
blusher	**blosser**	[blossər]
perfume (bottled)	**parfuum**	[parfɪm]
toilet water (lotion)	**reukwater**	[røək·vatər]
lotion	**vloeiroom**	[flui·roəm]
cologne	**reukwater**	[røək·vatər]
eyeshadow	**oogskadu**	[oəχ·skadu]
eyeliner	**oogomlyner**	[oəχ·omlajnər]
mascara	**maskara**	[maskara]
lipstick	**lipstiffie**	[lip·stiffi]
nail polish	**naellak**	[naɛl·lak]
hair spray	**haarsproei**	[hãrs·prui]
deodorant	**reukweermiddel**	[røək·veərmiddəl]
cream	**room**	[roəm]
face cream	**gesigroom**	[xesiχ·roəm]
hand cream	**handroom**	[hand·roəm]
anti-wrinkle cream	**antirimpelroom**	[antirimpəl·roəm]
day cream	**dagroom**	[daχ·roəm]
night cream	**nagroom**	[naχ·roəm]
day (as adj)	**dag-**	[daχ-]
night (as adj)	**nag-**	[naχ-]
tampon	**tampon**	[tampon]
toilet paper (toilet roll)	**toiletpapier**	[tojlet·papir]
hair dryer	**haardroër**	[hãr·droɛr]

39. Jewellery

jewellery, jewels	**juweliersware**	[juvelirs·warə]
precious (e.g. ~ stone)	**edel-**	[ɛdəl-]
hallmark stamp	**waarmerk**	[vãrmerk]
ring	**ring**	[riŋ]
wedding ring	**trouring**	[træʊriŋ]
bracelet	**armband**	[armbant]
earrings	**oorbelle**	[oər·bɛllə]

necklace (~ of pearls)	**halssnoer**	[hals·snur]
crown	**kroon**	[kroən]
bead necklace	**kraalsnoer**	[krāl·snur]

diamond	**diamant**	[diamant]
emerald	**smarag**	[smaraχ]
ruby	**robyn**	[robajn]
sapphire	**saffier**	[saffir]
pearl	**pêrel**	[pærəl]
amber	**amber**	[ambər]

40. Watches. Clocks

watch (wristwatch)	**polshorlosie**	[pols·horlosi]
dial	**wyserplaat**	[vajsər·plāt]
hand (clock, watch)	**wyster**	[vajstər]
metal bracelet	**metaal horlosiebandjie**	[metāl horlosi·bandʒi]
watch strap	**horlosiebandjie**	[horlosi·bandʒi]

battery	**battery**	[battəraj]
to be flat (battery)	**pap wees**	[pap veəs]
to run fast	**voorloop**	[foərloəp]
to run slow	**agterloop**	[aχtərloəp]

wall clock	**muurhorlosie**	[mɪr·horlosi]
hourglass	**uurglas**	[ɪr·χlas]
sundial	**sonwyser**	[son·wajsər]
alarm clock	**wekker**	[vɛkkər]
watchmaker	**horlosiemaker**	[horlosi·makər]
to repair (vt)	**herstel**	[herstəl]

Food. Nutricion

meat	vleis	[flæjs]
chicken	hoender	[hundər]
poussin	braaikuiken	[brāj·kœiken]
duck	eend	[eent]
goose	gans	[xaŋs]
game	wild	[vilt]
turkey	kalkoen	[kalkun]
pork	varkvleis	[fark·flæjs]
veal	kalfsvleis	[kalfs·flæjs]
lamb	lamsvleis	[lams·flæjs]
beef	beesvleis	[beəs·flæjs]
rabbit	konynvleis	[konajn·flæjs]
sausage (bologna, etc.)	wors	[vors]
vienna sausage (frankfurter)	Weense worsie	[veɛŋsə vorsi]
bacon	spek	[spek]
ham	ham	[ham]
gammon	gerookte ham	[xeroəktə ham]
pâté	patee	[pateə]
liver	lewer	[levər]
mince (minced meat)	maalvleis	[māl·flæjs]
tongue	tong	[toŋ]
egg	eier	[æjer]
eggs	eiers	[æjers]
egg white	eierwit	[æjer·wit]
egg yolk	dooier	[dojer]
fish	vis	[fis]
seafood	seekos	[seə·kos]
crustaceans	skaaldiere	[skāldirə]
caviar	kaviaar	[kafiār]
crab	krab	[krap]
prawn	garnaal	[xarnāl]
oyster	oester	[ustər]
spiny lobster	seekreef	[seə·kreəf]
octopus	seekat	[seə·kat]
squid	pylinkvis	[pajl·inkfis]
sturgeon	steur	[støər]
salmon	salm	[salm]
halibut	heilbot	[hæjlbot]
cod	kabeljou	[kabeljæʊ]

mackerel	makriel	[makril]
tuna	tuna	[tuna]
eel	paling	[paliŋ]

trout	forel	[forəl]
sardine	sardyn	[sardajn]
pike	varswatersnoek	[farswatər·snuk]
herring	haring	[hariŋ]

bread	brood	[broət]
cheese	kaas	[kās]
sugar	suiker	[sœikər]
salt	sout	[sæʊt]

rice	rys	[rajs]
pasta (macaroni)	pasta	[pasta]
noodles	noedels	[nudɛls]

butter	botter	[bottər]
vegetable oil	plantaardige olie	[plantārdiχə oli]
sunflower oil	sonblomolie	[sonblom·oli]
margarine	margarien	[marχarin]

| olives | olywe | [olajvə] |
| olive oil | olyfolie | [olajf·oli] |

milk	melk	[melk]
condensed milk	kondensmelk	[kondɛŋs·melk]
yogurt	jogurt	[joχurt]
soured cream	suurroom	[sɪr·roəm]
cream (of milk)	room	[roəm]

| mayonnaise | mayonnaise | [majonɛs] |
| buttercream | crème | [krɛm] |

groats (barley ~, etc.)	ontbytgraan	[ontbajt·χrān]
flour	meelblom	[meəl·blom]
tinned food	blikkieskos	[blikkis·kos]

cornflakes	mielievlokkies	[mili·flokkis]
honey	heuning	[høəniŋ]
jam	konfyt	[konfajt]
chewing gum	kougom	[kæʊχom]

42. Drinks

water	water	[vatər]
drinking water	drinkwater	[drink·vatər]
mineral water	mineraalwater	[minerāl·vatər]

still (adj)	sonder gas	[sondər χas]
carbonated (adj)	soda-	[soda-]
sparkling (adj)	bruis-	[brœis-]
ice	ys	[ajs]

with ice	met ys	[met ajs]
non-alcoholic (adj)	nie-alkoholies	[ni-alkoholis]
soft drink	koeldrank	[kul·drank]
refreshing drink	verfrissende drank	[ferfrissendə drank]
lemonade	limonade	[limonadə]

spirits	likeure	[likøərə]
wine	wyn	[vajn]
white wine	witwyn	[vit·vajn]
red wine	rooiwyn	[roj·vajn]

liqueur	likeur	[likøər]
champagne	sjampanje	[ʃampanje]
vermouth	vermoet	[fermut]

whisky	whisky	[vhiskaj]
vodka	vodka	[fodka]
gin	jenever	[jenefər]
cognac	brandewyn	[brandə·vajn]
rum	rum	[rum]

coffee	koffie	[koffi]
black coffee	swart koffie	[swart koffi]
white coffee	koffie met melk	[koffi met melk]
cappuccino	capuccino	[kaputʃino]
instant coffee	poeierkoffie	[pujer·koffi]

milk	melk	[melk]
cocktail	mengeldrankie	[menχəl·dranki]
milkshake	melkskommel	[melk·skomməl]

juice	sap	[sap]
tomato juice	tamatiesap	[tamati·sap]
orange juice	lemoensap	[lemoən·sap]
freshly squeezed juice	vars geparste sap	[fars χeparstə sap]

beer	bier	[bir]
lager	ligte bier	[liχtə bir]
bitter	donker bier	[donkər bir]

tea	tee	[teə]
black tea	swart tee	[swart teə]
green tea	groen tee	[χrun teə]

43. Vegetables

| vegetables | groente | [χruntə] |
| greens | groente | [χruntə] |

tomato	tamatie	[tamati]
cucumber	komkommer	[komkommər]
carrot	wortel	[vortəl]
potato	aartappel	[ārtappəl]
onion	ui	[œi]

garlic	knoffel	[knoffəl]
cabbage	kool	[koəl]
cauliflower	blomkool	[blom·koəl]
Brussels sprouts	Brusselspruite	[brussɛl·sprœitə]
broccoli	broccoli	[brokoli]

beetroot	beet	[beət]
aubergine	eiervrug	[æjerfruχ]
courgette	vingerskorsie	[fiŋər·skorsi]
pumpkin	pampoen	[pampun]
turnip	raap	[rãp]

parsley	pietersielie	[pitərsili]
dill	dille	[dillə]
lettuce	slaai	[slãi]
celery	seldery	[selderaj]
asparagus	aspersie	[aspersi]
spinach	spinasie	[spinasi]

pea	ertjie	[ɛrki]
beans	boontjies	[boənkis]
maize	mielie	[mili]
kidney bean	nierboontjie	[nir·boənki]

sweet paper	paprika	[paprika]
radish	radys	[radajs]
artichoke	artisjok	[artiʃok]

44. Fruits. Nuts

fruit	vrugte	[fruχtə]
apple	appel	[appəl]
pear	peer	[peər]
lemon	suurlemoen	[sɪr·lemun]
orange	lemoen	[lemun]
strawberry (garden ~)	aarbei	[ãrbæj]

tangerine	nartjie	[narki]
plum	pruim	[prœim]
peach	perske	[perskə]
apricot	appelkoos	[appɛlkoəs]
raspberry	framboos	[framboəs]
pineapple	pynappel	[pajnappəl]

banana	piesang	[pisaŋ]
watermelon	waatlemoen	[vãtlemun]
grape	druif	[drœif]
cherry	kersie	[kersi]
sour cherry	suurkersie	[sɪr·kersi]
sweet cherry	soetkersie	[sut·kersi]
melon	spanspek	[spaŋspek]

| grapefruit | pomelo | [pomelo] |
| avocado | avokado | [afokado] |

papaya	**papaja**	[papaja]
mango	**mango**	[manχo]
pomegranate	**granaat**	[χranãt]

redcurrant	**rooi aalbessie**	[roj ãlbɛssi]
blackcurrant	**swartbessie**	[swartbɛssi]
gooseberry	**appelliefie**	[appɛllifi]
bilberry	**bosbessie**	[bosbɛssi]
blackberry	**braambessie**	[brãmbɛssi]

raisin	**rosyntjie**	[rosajnki]
fig	**vy**	[faj]
date	**dadel**	[dadəl]

peanut	**grondboontjie**	[χront·boənki]
almond	**amandel**	[amandəl]
walnut	**okkerneut**	[okkər·nøət]
hazelnut	**haselneut**	[hasɛl·nøət]
coconut	**klapper**	[klappər]
pistachios	**pistachio**	[pistatʃio]

45. Bread. Sweets

bakers' confectionery (pastry)	**soet gebak**	[sut χebak]
bread	**brood**	[broət]
biscuits	**koekies**	[kukis]

chocolate (n)	**sjokolade**	[ʃokoladə]
chocolate (as adj)	**sjokolade**	[ʃokoladə]
candy (wrapped)	**lekkers**	[lɛkkərs]
cake (e.g. cupcake)	**koek**	[kuk]
cake (e.g. birthday ~)	**koek**	[kuk]

| pie (e.g. apple ~) | **pastei** | [pastæj] |
| filling (for cake, pie) | **vulsel** | [fulsəl] |

jam (whole fruit jam)	**konfyt**	[konfajt]
marmalade	**marmelade**	[marmeladə]
wafers	**wafels**	[vafɛls]
ice-cream	**roomys**	[roəm·ajs]
pudding (Christmas ~)	**poeding**	[pudiŋ]

46. Cooked dishes

course, dish	**gereg**	[χerəχ]
cuisine	**kookkuns**	[koək·kuns]
recipe	**resep**	[resep]
portion	**porsie**	[porsi]

salad	**slaai**	[slãi]
soup	**sop**	[sop]
clear soup (broth)	**helder sop**	[hɛldər sop]

| sandwich (bread) | toebroodjie | [tubroədʒi] |
| fried eggs | gabakte eiers | [χabaktə æjers] |

| hamburger (beefburger) | hamburger | [hamburχər] |
| beefsteak | biefstuk | [bifstuk] |

side dish	sygereg	[saj·χerəχ]
spaghetti	spaghetti	[spaχɛtti]
mash	kapokaartappels	[kapok·ārtappəls]
pizza	pizza	[pizza]
porridge (oatmeal, etc.)	pap	[pap]
omelette	omelet	[oməlet]

boiled (e.g. ~ beef)	gekook	[χekoək]
smoked (adj)	gerook	[χeroək]
fried (adj)	gebak	[χebak]
dried (adj)	gedroog	[χedroəχ]
frozen (adj)	gevries	[χefris]
pickled (adj)	gepiekel	[χepikəl]

sweet (sugary)	soet	[sut]
salty (adj)	sout	[sæʊt]
cold (adj)	koud	[kæʊt]
hot (adj)	warm	[varm]
bitter (adj)	bitter	[bittər]
tasty (adj)	smaaklik	[smāklik]

to cook in boiling water	kook in water	[koək in vatər]
to cook (dinner)	kook	[koək]
to fry (vt)	braai	[braj]
to heat up (food)	opwarm	[opwarm]

to salt (vt)	sout	[sæʊt]
to pepper (vt)	peper	[pepər]
to grate (vt)	rasp	[rasp]
peel (n)	skil	[skil]
to peel (vt)	skil	[skil]

47. Spices

salt	sout	[sæʊt]
salty (adj)	sout	[sæʊt]
to salt (vt)	sout	[sæʊt]

black pepper	swart peper	[swart pepər]
red pepper (milled ~)	rooi peper	[roj pepər]
mustard	mosterd	[mostert]
horseradish	peperwortel	[peper·wortəl]

condiment	smaakmiddel	[smāk·middəl]
spice	spesery	[spesəraj]
sauce	sous	[sæʊs]
vinegar	asyn	[asajn]
anise	anys	[anajs]

basil	basilikum	[basilikum]
cloves	naeltjies	[naɛlkis]
ginger	gemmer	[χɛmmər]
coriander	koljander	[koljandər]
cinnamon	kaneel	[kaneəl]

sesame	sesamsaad	[sesam·sãt]
bay leaf	lourierblaar	[læurir·blãr]
paprika	paprika	[paprika]
caraway	komynsaad	[komajnsãt]
saffron	saffraan	[saffrãn]

48. Meals

| food | kos | [kos] |
| to eat (vi, vt) | eet | [eət] |

breakfast	ontbyt	[ontbajt]
to have breakfast	ontbyt	[ontbajt]
lunch	middagete	[middaχ·etə]
to have lunch	gaan eet	[χãn eət]
dinner	aandete	[ãndetə]
to have dinner	aandete gebruik	[ãndetə χebrœik]

| appetite | aptyt | [aptajt] |
| Enjoy your meal! | Smaaklike ete! | [smãklikə etə!] |

to open (~ a bottle)	oopmaak	[oəpmãk]
to spill (liquid)	mors	[mors]
to spill out (vi)	mors	[mors]

to boil (vi)	kook	[koək]
to boil (vt)	kook	[koək]
boiled (~ water)	gekook	[χekoək]
to chill, cool down (vt)	laat afkoel	[lãt afkul]
to chill (vi)	afkoel	[afkul]

| taste, flavour | smaak | [smãk] |
| aftertaste | nasmaak | [nasmãk] |

to slim down (lose weight)	vermaer	[fermaər]
diet	dieet	[diət]
vitamin	vitamien	[fitamin]
calorie	kalorie	[kalori]
vegetarian (n)	vegetariër	[feχetariɛr]
vegetarian (adj)	vegetaries	[feχetaris]

fats (nutrient)	vette	[fɛttə]
proteins	proteïen	[proteïen]
carbohydrates	koolhidrate	[koəlhidratə]

slice (of lemon, ham)	snytjie	[snajki]
piece (of cake, pie)	stuk	[stuk]
crumb (of bread, cake, etc.)	krummel	[krumməl]

49. Table setting

spoon	lepel	[lepəl]
knife	mes	[mes]
fork	vurk	[furk]

cup (e.g., coffee ~)	koppie	[koppi]
plate (dinner ~)	bord	[bort]
saucer	piering	[piriŋ]
serviette	servet	[serfət]
toothpick	tandestokkie	[tandə·stokki]

50. Restaurant

restaurant	restaurant	[restɔurant]
coffee bar	koffiekroeg	[koffi·kruχ]
pub, bar	kroeg	[kruχ]
tearoom	teekamer	[teə·kamər]

waiter	kelner	[kɛlnər]
waitress	kelnerin	[kɛlnərin]
barman	kroegman	[kruχman]

menu	spyskaart	[spajs·kārt]
wine list	wyn	[vajn]
to book a table	wynkaart	[vajn·kārt]

course, dish	gereg	[χerəχ]
to order (meal)	bestel	[bestəl]
to make an order	bestel	[bestəl]

aperitif	drankie	[dranki]
starter	voorgereg	[foərχerəχ]
dessert, pudding	nagereg	[naχerəχ]

bill	rekening	[rekəniŋ]
to pay the bill	die rekening betaal	[di rekeniŋ betāl]
to give change	kleingeld gee	[klæjn·χɛlt χeə]
tip	fooitjie	[fojki]

Family, relatives and friends

51. Personal information. Forms

name (first name)	**voornaam**	[foərnãm]
surname (last name)	**van**	[fan]
date of birth	**geboortedatum**	[χeboərtə·datum]
place of birth	**geboorteplek**	[χeboərtə·plek]
nationality	**nasionaliteit**	[naʃionalitæjt]
place of residence	**woonplek**	[voən·plek]
country	**land**	[lant]
profession (occupation)	**beroep**	[berup]
gender, sex	**geslag**	[χeslaχ]
height	**lengte**	[leŋtə]
weight	**gewig**	[χevəχ]

52. Family members. Relatives

mother	**moeder**	[mudər]
father	**vader**	[fadər]
son	**seun**	[søən]
daughter	**dogter**	[doχtər]
younger daughter	**jonger dogter**	[joŋər doχtər]
younger son	**jonger seun**	[joŋər søən]
eldest daughter	**oudste dogter**	[æudstə doχtər]
eldest son	**oudste seun**	[æudstə søən]
brother	**broer**	[brur]
elder brother	**ouer broer**	[æuer brur]
younger brother	**jonger broer**	[joŋər brur]
sister	**suster**	[sustər]
elder sister	**ouer suster**	[æuer sustər]
younger sister	**jonger suster**	[joŋər sustər]
cousin (masc.)	**neef**	[neəf]
cousin (fem.)	**neef**	[neəf]
mummy	**ma**	[ma]
dad, daddy	**pa**	[pa]
parents	**ouers**	[æuers]
child	**kind**	[kint]
children	**kinders**	[kindərs]
grandmother	**ouma**	[æuma]
grandfather	**oupa**	[æupa]

grandson	kleinseun	[klæjn·søən]
granddaughter	kleindogter	[klæjn·doχtər]
grandchildren	kleinkinders	[klæjn·kindərs]

uncle	oom	[oəm]
aunt	tante	[tantə]
nephew	neef	[neəf]
niece	nig	[niχ]

mother-in-law (wife's mother)	skoonma	[skoən·ma]
father-in-law (husband's father)	skoonpa	[skoən·pa]
son-in-law (daughter's husband)	skoonseun	[skoən·søən]
stepmother	stiefma	[stifma]
stepfather	stiefpa	[stifpa]

infant	baba	[baba]
baby (infant)	baba	[baba]
little boy, kid	seuntjie	[søənki]

wife	vrou	[fræʋ]
husband	man	[man]
spouse (husband)	eggenoot	[εχχenoət]
spouse (wife)	eggenote	[εχχenotə]

married (masc.)	getroud	[χetræʋt]
married (fem.)	getroud	[χetræʋt]
single (unmarried)	ongetroud	[onχetræʋt]
bachelor	vrygesel	[frajχesəl]
divorced (masc.)	geskei	[χeskæj]
widow	weduwee	[veduveə]
widower	wedunaar	[vedunãr]

relative	familielid	[famililit]
close relative	na familie	[na famili]
distant relative	ver familie	[fer famili]
relatives	familielede	[famililedə]

orphan (boy or girl)	weeskind	[veəskint]
guardian (of a minor)	voog	[foəχ]
to adopt (a boy)	aanneem	[ãnneəm]
to adopt (a girl)	aanneem	[ãnneəm]

53. Friends. Colleagues

friend (masc.)	vriend	[frint]
friend (fem.)	vriendin	[frindin]
friendship	vriendskap	[frindskap]
to be friends	bevriend wees	[befrint veəs]

| pal (masc.) | maat | [mãt] |
| pal (fem.) | vriendin | [frindin] |

partner	maat	[mãt]
chief (boss)	baas	[bãs]
superior (n)	baas	[bãs]
owner, proprietor	eienaar	[æjenãr]
subordinate (n)	ondergeskikte	[ondərχeskiktə]
colleague	kollega	[kolleχa]

acquaintance (person)	kennis	[kɛnnis]
fellow traveller	medereisiger	[medə·ræjsiχər]
classmate	klasmaat	[klas·mãt]

neighbour (masc.)	buurman	[bɪrman]
neighbour (fem.)	buurvrou	[bɪrfræʊ]
neighbours	bure	[burə]

54. Man. Woman

woman	vrou	[fræʊ]
girl (young woman)	meisie	[mæjsi]
bride	bruid	[brœit]

beautiful (adj)	mooi	[moj]
tall (adj)	groot	[χroət]
slender (adj)	slank	[slank]
short (adj)	kort	[kort]

blonde (n)	blondine	[blondinə]
brunette (n)	brunet	[brunet]
ladies' (adj)	dames-	[dames-]
virgin (girl)	maagd	[mãχt]
pregnant (adj)	swanger	[swaŋər]

man (adult male)	man	[man]
blonde haired man	blond	[blont]
dark haired man	brunet	[brunet]
tall (adj)	groot	[χroət]
short (adj)	kort	[kort]
rude (rough)	onbeskof	[onbeskof]
stocky (adj)	frisgebou	[frisχebæʊ]
robust (adj)	frisgebou	[frisχebæʊ]
strong (adj)	sterk	[sterk]
strength	sterkte	[sterktə]

plump, fat (adj)	vet	[fet]
swarthy (dark-skinned)	blas	[blas]
slender (well-built)	slank	[slank]
elegant (adj)	elegant	[ɛleχant]

55. Age

| age | ouderdom | [æʊderdom] |
| youth (young age) | jeug | [jøəχ] |

young (adj)	jong	[joŋ]
younger (adj)	jonger	[joŋər]
older (adj)	ouer	[æʋer]

young man	jongman	[joŋman]
teenager	tiener	[tinər]
guy, fellow	ou	[æʋ]

| old man | ou man | [æʋ man] |
| old woman | ou vrou | [æʋ fræʋ] |

adult (adj)	volwasse	[folwassə]
middle-aged (adj)	middeljarig	[middəl·jarəχ]
elderly (adj)	bejaard	[bejãrt]
old (adj)	oud	[æʋt]

retirement	pensioen	[pɛnsiun]
to retire (from job)	met pensioen gaan	[met pɛnsiun χãn]
retiree, pensioner	pensioenaris	[pɛnsiunaris]

56. Children

child	kind	[kint]
children	kinders	[kindərs]
twins	tweeling	[tweəliŋ]

cradle	wiegie	[viχi]
rattle	rammelaar	[rammelãr]
nappy	luier	[lœiər]

dummy, comforter	fopspeen	[fopspeən]
pram	kinderwaentjie	[kindər·waenki]
nursery	kindertuin	[kindər·tœin]
babysitter	babasitter	[babasittər]

childhood	kinderdae	[kindərdaə]
doll	pop	[pop]
toy	speelgoed	[speəl·χut]
construction set (toy)	boudoos	[bæʋ·doəs]
well-bred (adj)	goed opgevoed	[χut opχəfut]
ill-bred (adj)	sleg opgevoed	[sleχ opχəfut]
spoilt (adj)	bederf	[bederf]

to be naughty	stout wees	[stæʋt veəs]
mischievous (adj)	ondeuend	[ondøent]
mischievousness	ondeuendheid	[ondøenthæjt]
mischievous child	rakker	[rakkər]

| obedient (adj) | gehoorsaam | [χehoərsãm] |
| disobedient (adj) | ongehoorsaam | [onχəhoərsãm] |

docile (adj)	soet	[sut]
clever (intelligent)	slim	[slim]
child prodigy	wonderkind	[vondərkint]

57. Married couples. Family life

to kiss (vt)	soen	[sun]
to kiss (vi)	mekaar soen	[mekār sun]
family (n)	familie	[famili]
family (as adj)	gesins-	[χesins-]
couple	paartjie	[pārki]
marriage (state)	huwelik	[huvelik]
hearth (home)	tuiste	[tœistə]
dynasty	dinastie	[dinasti]
date	datum	[datum]
kiss	soen	[sun]
love (for sb)	liefde	[lifdə]
to love (sb)	liefhê	[lifhɛ:]
beloved	geliefde	[χelifdə]
tenderness	teerheid	[teərhæjt]
tender (affectionate)	teer	[teər]
faithfulness	trou	[træʋ]
faithful (adj)	trou	[træʋ]
care (attention)	sorg	[sorχ]
caring (~ father)	sorgsaam	[sorχsām]
newlyweds	pasgetroudes	[pas·χetræʋdes]
honeymoon	wittebroodsdae	[vittebroəds·daə]
to get married (ab. woman)	trou	[træʋ]
to get married (ab. man)	trou	[træʋ]
wedding	bruilof	[brœilof]
golden wedding	goue bruilof	[χæʋə brœilof]
anniversary	verjaardag	[ferjār·daχ]
lover (masc.)	minnaar	[minnār]
mistress (lover)	minnares	[minnares]
adultery	owerspel	[overspəl]
to cheat on ... (commit adultery)	owerspel pleeg	[overspəl pleeχ]
jealous (adj)	jaloers	[jalurs]
to be jealous	jaloers wees	[jalurs veəs]
divorce	egskeiding	[ɛχskæjdiŋ]
to divorce (vi)	skei	[skæj]
to quarrel (vi)	baklei	[baklæj]
to be reconciled (after an argument)	versoen	[fersun]
together (adv)	saam	[sām]
sex	seks	[seks]
happiness	geluk	[χeluk]
happy (adj)	gelukkig	[χelukkəχ]
misfortune (accident)	ongeluk	[onχəluk]
unhappy (adj)	ongelukkig	[onχəlukkəχ]

Character. Feelings. Emotions

58. Feelings. Emotions

feeling (emotion)	gevoel	[χeful]
feelings	gevoelens	[χefulɛŋs]
to feel (vt)	voel	[ful]
hunger	honger	[hoŋər]
to be hungry	honger wees	[hoŋər veəs]
thirst	dors	[dors]
to be thirsty	dors wees	[dors veəs]
sleepiness	slaperigheid	[slaperiχæjt]
to feel sleepy	vaak voel	[fāk ful]
tiredness	moegheid	[muχæjt]
tired (adj)	moeg	[muχ]
to get tired	moeg word	[muχ vort]
mood (humour)	stemming	[stɛmmiŋ]
boredom	verveling	[ferfeliŋ]
to be bored	verveeld wees	[ferveəlt veəs]
seclusion	afsondering	[afsondəriŋ]
to seclude oneself	jou afsonder	[jæu afsondər]
to worry (make anxious)	bekommerd maak	[bekommərt māk]
to be worried	bekommerd wees	[bekommərt veəs]
worrying (n)	kommerwekkend	[kommər·wɛkkent]
anxiety	vrees	[freəs]
preoccupied (adj)	behep	[behep]
to be nervous	senuweeagtig wees	[senuveə·aχtəχ veəs]
to panic (vi)	paniekerig raak	[panikerəχ rāk]
hope	hoop	[hoəp]
to hope (vi, vt)	hoop	[hoəp]
certainty	sekerheid	[sekərhæjt]
certain, sure (adj)	seker	[sekər]
uncertainty	onsekerheid	[ɔŋsekərhæjt]
uncertain (adj)	onseker	[ɔŋsekər]
drunk (adj)	dronk	[dronk]
sober (adj)	nugter	[nuχtər]
weak (adj)	swak	[swak]
happy (adj)	gelukkig	[χelukkəχ]
to scare (vt)	bang maak	[baŋ māk]
fury (madness)	kwaadheid	[kwādhæjt]
rage (fury)	woede	[vudə]
depression	depressie	[deprɛssi]
discomfort (unease)	ongemak	[ɔnχəmak]

comfort	gemak	[χemak]
to regret (be sorry)	jammer wees	[jammər veəs]
regret	spyt	[spajt]
bad luck	teëspoed	[teɛsput]
sadness	droefheid	[drufhæjt]

shame (remorse)	skaamte	[skāmtə]
gladness	vreugde	[frøəχdə]
enthusiasm, zeal	entoesiasme	[ɛntusiasmə]
enthusiast	entoesiasties	[ɛntusiastis]
to show enthusiasm	begeestering toon	[beχeəsteriɲ toən]

59. Character. Personality

character	karakter	[karaktər]
character flaw	karakterfout	[karaktər·fæut]
mind	verstand	[ferstant]
reason	verstand	[ferstant]

conscience	gewete	[χevetə]
habit (custom)	gewoonte	[χevoentə]
ability (talent)	talent	[talent]
can (e.g. ~ swim)	kan	[kan]

patient (adj)	geduldig	[χeduldəχ]
impatient (adj)	ongeduldig	[onχeduldəχ]
curious (inquisitive)	nuuskierig	[nɪskirəχ]
curiosity	nuuskierigheid	[nɪskiriχæjt]

modesty	beskeidenheid	[beskæjdenhæjt]
modest (adj)	beskeie	[beskæje]
immodest (adj)	onbeskeie	[onbeskæje]

laziness	luiheid	[lœihæjt]
lazy (adj)	lui	[lœi]
lazy person (masc.)	luiaard	[lœiārt]

cunning (n)	sluheid	[sluhæjt]
cunning (as adj)	slu	[slu]
distrust	wantroue	[vantræuə]
distrustful (adj)	agterdogtig	[aχtərdoχtəχ]

generosity	gulheid	[χulhæjt]
generous (adj)	gulhartig	[χulhartəχ]
talented (adj)	talentvol	[talentfol]
talent	talent	[talent]

courageous (adj)	moedig	[mudəχ]
courage	moed	[mut]
honest (adj)	eerlik	[eərlik]
honesty	eerlikheid	[eərlikhæjt]

| careful (cautious) | versigtig | [fersiχtəχ] |
| brave (courageous) | dapper | [dappər] |

| serious (adj) | ernstig | [ɛrnstəχ] |
| strict (severe, stern) | streng | [streŋ] |

decisive (adj)	vasberade	[fasberadə]
indecisive (adj)	besluiteloos	[beslœiteloəs]
shy, timid (adj)	skaam	[skãm]
shyness, timidity	skaamheid	[skãmhæjt]

confidence (trust)	vertroue	[fertræʊə]
to believe (trust)	vertrou	[fertræʊ]
trusting (credulous)	goedgelowig	[χudχəlovəχ]

sincerely (adv)	opreg	[opreχ]
sincere (adj)	opregte	[opreχtə]
sincerity	opregtheid	[opreχthæjt]
open (person)	oop	[oəp]

calm (adj)	kalm	[kalm]
frank (sincere)	openhartig	[openhartəχ]
naïve (adj)	naïef	[naïef]
absent-minded (adj)	verstrooid	[ferstrojt]
funny (odd)	snaaks	[snãks]

greed, stinginess	hebsug	[hebsuχ]
greedy, stingy (adj)	hebsugtig	[hebsuχtəχ]
stingy (adj)	gierig	[χirəχ]
evil (adj)	boos	[boəs]
stubborn (adj)	hardnekkig	[hardnɛkkəχ]
unpleasant (adj)	onaangenaam	[onãnχənãm]

selfish person (masc.)	selfsugtig	[sɛlfsuχtəχ]
selfish (adj)	selfsugtig	[sɛlfsuχtəχ]
coward	laffaard	[laffãrt]
cowardly (adj)	lafhartig	[lafhartəχ]

60. Sleep. Dreams

to sleep (vi)	slaap	[slãp]
sleep, sleeping	slaap	[slãp]
dream	droom	[droəm]
to dream (in sleep)	droom	[droəm]
sleepy (adj)	vaak	[fãk]

bed	bed	[bet]
mattress	matras	[matras]
blanket (eiderdown)	kombers	[kombers]
pillow	kussing	[kussiŋ]
sheet	laken	[laken]

insomnia	slaaploosheid	[slãploəshæjt]
sleepless (adj)	slaaploos	[slãploəs]
sleeping pill	slaappil	[slãp·pil]
to feel sleepy	vaak voel	[fãk ful]
to yawn (vi)	gaap	[χãp]

to go to bed	**gaan slaap**	[χān slāp]
to make up the bed	**die bed opmaak**	[di bet opmāk]
to fall asleep	**aan die slaap raak**	[ān di slāp rāk]
nightmare	**nagmerrie**	[naχmerri]
snore, snoring	**gesnork**	[χesnork]
to snore (vi)	**snork**	[snork]
alarm clock	**wekker**	[vɛkkər]
to wake (vt)	**wakker maak**	[vakkər māk]
to wake up	**wakker word**	[vakkər vort]
to get up (vi)	**opstaan**	[opstān]
to have a wash	**jou was**	[jæʊ vas]

61. Humour. Laughter. Gladness

humour (wit, fun)	**humor**	[humor]
sense of humour	**humorsin**	[humorsin]
to enjoy oneself	**jouself geniet**	[jæʊsɛlf χenit]
cheerful (merry)	**vrolik**	[frolik]
merriment (gaiety)	**pret**	[pret]
smile	**glimlag**	[χlimlaχ]
to smile (vi)	**glimlag**	[χlimlaχ]
to start laughing	**begin lag**	[beχin laχ]
to laugh (vi)	**lag**	[laχ]
laugh, laughter	**lag**	[laχ]
anecdote	**anekdote**	[anekdotə]
funny (anecdote, etc.)	**snaaks**	[snāks]
funny (odd)	**snaaks**	[snāks]
to joke (vi)	**grappies maak**	[χrappis māk]
joke (verbal)	**grappie**	[χrappi]
joy (emotion)	**vreugde**	[frøəχdə]
to rejoice (vi)	**bly wees**	[blaj veəs]
joyful (adj)	**bly**	[blaj]

62. Discussion, conversation. Part 1

communication	**kommunikasie**	[kommunikasi]
to communicate	**kommunikeer**	[kommunikeər]
conversation	**gesprek**	[χesprek]
dialogue	**dialoog**	[dialoəχ]
discussion (discourse)	**diskussie**	[diskussi]
dispute (debate)	**dispuut**	[dispɪt]
to dispute, to debate	**debatteer**	[debatteər]
interlocutor	**gespreksgenoot**	[χespreks·χenoət]
topic (theme)	**onderwerp**	[ondərwerp]
point of view	**standpunt**	[stand·punt]

| opinion (point of view) | opinie | [opini] |
| speech (talk) | toespraak | [tusprãk] |

discussion (of a report, etc.)	bespreking	[besprekiŋ]
to discuss (vt)	bespreek	[bespreək]
talk (conversation)	gesprek	[χesprek]
to talk (to chat)	gesels	[χesɛls]
meeting (encounter)	ontmoeting	[ontmutiŋ]
to meet (vi, vt)	ontmoet	[ontmut]

proverb	spreekwoord	[spreək·woərt]
saying	gesegde	[χeseχdə]
riddle (poser)	raaisel	[rãjsəl]
password	wagwoord	[vaχ·woərt]
secret	geheim	[χəhæjm]

oath (vow)	eed	[eət]
to swear (an oath)	sweer	[sweər]
promise	belofte	[beloftə]
to promise (vt)	beloof	[beloəf]

advice (counsel)	raad	[rãt]
to advise (vt)	aanraai	[ãnrãi]
to follow one's advice	raad volg	[rãt folχ]
to listen to ... (obey)	luister na	[lœistər na]

news	nuus	[nɪs]
sensation (news)	sensasie	[sɛŋsasi]
information (report)	inligting	[inliχtiŋ]
conclusion (decision)	slotsom	[slotsom]
voice	stem	[stem]
compliment	kompliment	[kompliment]
kind (nice)	gaaf	[χãf]

word	woord	[voərt]
phrase	frase	[frasə]
answer	antwoord	[antwoərt]

| truth | waarheid | [vãrhæjt] |
| lie | leuen | [løəen] |

thought	gedagte	[χedaχtə]
idea (inspiration)	idee	[ideə]
fantasy	verbeelding	[ferbeəldiŋ]

63. Discussion, conversation. Part 2

respected (adj)	gerespekteer	[χerespekteər]
to respect (vt)	respekteer	[respekteər]
respect	respek	[respek]
Dear ... (letter)	Geagte ...	[χeaχtə ...]

| to introduce (sb to sb) | voorstel | [foərstəl] |
| to make acquaintance | kennismaak | [kɛnnismãk] |

intention	voorneme	[foərnemə]
to intend (have in mind)	voornemens wees	[foərneməŋs veəs]
wish	wens	[vɛŋs]
to wish (~ good luck)	wens	[vɛŋs]

surprise (astonishment)	verrassing	[ferrassiŋ]
to surprise (amaze)	verras	[ferras]
to be surprised	verbaas wees	[ferbãs veəs]

to give (vt)	gee	[χeə]
to take (get hold of)	vat	[fat]
to give back	teruggee	[teruχeə]
to return (give back)	terugvat	[teruχfat]

to apologize (vi)	verskoning vra	[ferskoniŋ fra]
apology	verskoning	[ferskoniŋ]
to forgive (vt)	vergewe	[ferχevə]

to talk (speak)	praat	[prãt]
to listen (vi)	luister	[lœistər]
to hear out	aanhoor	[ãnhoər]
to understand (vt)	verstaan	[ferstãn]
to show (to display)	wys	[vajs]
to look at ...	kyk na ...	[kajk na ...]
to call (yell for sb)	roep	[rup]
to distract (disturb)	aflei	[aflæj]
to disturb (vt)	steur	[støər]
to pass (to hand sth)	deurgee	[døərχeə]

demand (request)	versoek	[fersuk]
to request (ask)	versoek	[fersuk]
demand (firm request)	eis	[æjs]
to demand (request firmly)	eis	[æjs]

to tease (call names)	terg	[terχ]
to mock (make fun of)	terg	[terχ]
mockery, derision	spot	[spot]
nickname	bynaam	[bajnãm]

insinuation	sinspeling	[sinspeliŋ]
to insinuate (imply)	sinspeel	[sinspeəl]
to mean (vt)	impliseer	[impliseər]

description	beskrywing	[beskrajviŋ]
to describe (vt)	beskryf	[beskrajf]
praise (compliments)	lof	[lof]
to praise (vt)	loof	[loəf]

disappointment	teleurstelling	[teløərstɛlliŋ]
to disappoint (vt)	teleurstel	[teløərstəl]
to be disappointed	teleurgestel	[teløərχestəl]

supposition	veronderstelling	[feronderstɛlliŋ]
to suppose (assume)	veronderstel	[feronderstəl]
warning (caution)	waarskuwing	[vãrskuviŋ]
to warn (vt)	waarsku	[vãrsku]

64. Discussion, conversation. Part 3

to talk into (convince)	ompraat	[omprãt]
to calm down (vt)	kalmeer	[kalmeər]
silence (~ is golden)	stilte	[stiltə]
to be silent (not speaking)	stilbly	[stilblaj]
to whisper (vi, vt)	fluister	[flœistər]
whisper	gefluister	[χeflœistər]
frankly, sincerely (adv)	openlik	[openlik]
in my opinion ...	volgens my ...	[folχɛŋs maj ...]
detail (of the story)	besonderhede	[besondərhedə]
detailed (adj)	gedetailleerd	[χedetajlleərt]
in detail (adv)	in detail	[in detajl]
hint, clue	wenk	[vɛnk]
look (glance)	kykie	[kajki]
to have a look	kyk	[kajk]
fixed (look)	strak	[strak]
to blink (vi)	knipper	[knippər]
to wink (vi)	knipoog	[knipoəχ]
to nod (in assent)	knik	[knik]
sigh	sug	[suχ]
to sigh (vi)	sug	[suχ]
to shudder (vi)	huiwer	[hœivər]
gesture	gebaar	[χebãr]
to touch (one's arm, etc.)	aanraak	[ãnrãk]
to seize (e.g., ~ by the arm)	vat	[fat]
to tap (on the shoulder)	op die skouer tik	[op di skæuər tik]
Look out!	Oppas!	[oppas!]
Really?	Regtig?	[reχtəχ?]
Are you sure?	Is jy seker?	[is jaj sekər?]
Good luck!	Voorspoed!	[foərspud!]
I see!	Ek sien!	[ɛk sin!]
What a pity!	Jammer!	[jammər!]

65. Agreement. Refusal

consent	toelating	[tulatiŋ]
to consent (vi)	toelaat	[tulãt]
approval	goedkeuring	[χudkøəriŋ]
to approve (vt)	goedkeur	[χudkøər]
refusal	weiering	[væjeriŋ]
to refuse (vi, vt)	weier	[væjer]
Great!	Wonderlik!	[vondərlik!]
All right!	Goed!	[χud!]
Okay! (I agree)	OK!	[okej!]
forbidden (adj)	verbode	[ferbodə]

it's forbidden	**dit is verbode**	[dit is ferbodə]
it's impossible	**dis onmoontlik**	[dis onmoentlik]
incorrect (adj)	**onjuis**	[onjœis]
to reject (~ a demand)	**verwerp**	[ferwerp]
to support (cause, idea)	**steun**	[støən]
to accept (~ an apology)	**aanvaar**	[ānfār]
to confirm (vt)	**bevestig**	[befestəχ]
confirmation	**bevestiging**	[befestəχiŋ]
permission	**toelating**	[tulatiŋ]
to permit (vt)	**toelaat**	[tulāt]
decision	**besluit**	[beslœit]
to say nothing (hold one's tongue)	**stilbly**	[stilblaj]
condition (term)	**voorwaarde**	[foərwārdə]
excuse (pretext)	**verskoning**	[ferskoniŋ]
praise (compliments)	**lof**	[lof]
to praise (vt)	**loof**	[loəf]

66. Success. Good luck. Failure

success	**sukses**	[suksɛs]
successfully (adv)	**suksesvol**	[suksɛsfol]
successful (adj)	**suksesvol**	[suksɛsfol]
luck (good luck)	**geluk**	[χeluk]
Good luck!	**Voorspoed!**	[foərspud!]
lucky (e.g. ~ day)	**geluks-**	[χeluks-]
lucky (fortunate)	**gelukkig**	[χelukkəχ]
failure	**mislukking**	[mislukkiŋ]
misfortune	**teëspoed**	[teɛsput]
bad luck	**teëspoed**	[teɛsput]
unsuccessful (adj)	**onsuksesvol**	[ɔŋsuksɛsfol]
catastrophe	**katastrofe**	[katastrofə]
pride	**trots**	[trots]
proud (adj)	**trots**	[trots]
to be proud	**trots wees**	[trots veəs]
winner	**wenner**	[vɛnnər]
to win (vi)	**wen**	[ven]
to lose (not win)	**verloor**	[ferloər]
try	**probeerslag**	[probeərslaχ]
to try (vi)	**probeer**	[probeər]
chance (opportunity)	**kans**	[kaŋs]

67. Quarrels. Negative emotions

shout (scream)	**skreeu**	[skriʋ]
to shout (vi)	**skreeu**	[skriʋ]

to start to cry out	begin skreeu	[beχin skriʊ]
quarrel	rusie	[rusi]
to quarrel (vi)	baklei	[baklæj]
fight (squabble)	stryery	[strajeraj]
to make a scene	spektakel maak	[spektakəl māk]
conflict	konflik	[konflik]
misunderstanding	misverstand	[misferstant]

insult	belediging	[beledəχiŋ]
to insult (vt)	beledig	[beledəχ]
insulted (adj)	beledig	[beledəχ]
resentment	gekrenktheid	[χekrɛnkthæjt]
to offend (vt)	beledig	[beledəχ]
to take offence	gekrenk voel	[χekrɛnk ful]

indignation	verontwaardiging	[ferontwārdəχiŋ]
to be indignant	verontwaardig wees	[ferontwārdəχ veəs]
complaint	klag	[klaχ]
to complain (vi, vt)	kla	[kla]

apology	verskoning	[ferskoniŋ]
to apologize (vi)	verskoning vra	[ferskoniŋ fra]
to beg pardon	om verskoning vra	[om ferskoniŋ fra]

criticism	kritiek	[kritik]
to criticize (vt)	kritiseer	[kritiseər]
accusation (charge)	beskuldiging	[beskuldəχiŋ]
to accuse (vt)	beskuldig	[beskuldəχ]

revenge	wraak	[vrāk]
to avenge (get revenge)	wreek	[vreək]
to pay back	wraak neem	[vrāk neəm]

disdain	minagting	[minaχtiŋ]
to despise (vt)	minag	[minaχ]
hatred, hate	haat	[hāt]
to hate (vt)	haat	[hāt]

nervous (adj)	senuweeagtig	[senuveə·aχtəχ]
to be nervous	senuweeagtig wees	[senuveə·aχtəχ veəs]
angry (mad)	kwaad	[kwāt]
to make angry	kwaad maak	[kwāt māk]

humiliation	vernedering	[fernedəriŋ]
to humiliate (vt)	verneder	[fernedər]
to humiliate oneself	jouself verneder	[jæʊsɛlf fernedər]

| shock | skok | [skok] |
| to shock (vt) | skok | [skok] |

| trouble (e.g. serious ~) | probleme | [probləmə] |
| unpleasant (adj) | onaangenaam | [onānχənām] |

fear (dread)	vrees	[freəs]
terrible (storm, heat)	verskriklik	[ferskriklik]
scary (e.g. ~ story)	vreesaanjaend	[freəsānjaent]

| horror | afgryse | [afχrajsə] |
| awful (crime, news) | vreeslik | [freəslik] |

to begin to tremble	begin beef	[beχin beəf]
to cry (weep)	huil	[hœil]
to start crying	begin huil	[beχin hœil]
tear	traan	[trãn]

fault	skuld	[skult]
guilt (feeling)	skuldgevoel	[skultχəful]
dishonor (disgrace)	skande	[skandə]
protest	protes	[protes]
stress	stres	[stres]

to disturb (vt)	steur	[støər]
to be furious	woedend wees	[vudent veəs]
angry (adj)	kwaad	[kwãt]
to end (~ a relationship)	beëindig	[beεindəχ]
to swear (at sb)	sweer	[sweər]

to scare (become afraid)	skrik	[skrik]
to hit (strike with hand)	slaan	[slãn]
to fight (street fight, etc.)	baklei	[baklæj]

to settle (a conflict)	besleg	[besleχ]
discontented (adj)	ontevrede	[ontefredə]
furious (adj)	woedend	[vudent]

| It's not good! | Dis nie goed nie! | [dis ni χut ni!] |
| It's bad! | Dis sleg! | [dis sleχ!] |

Medicine

illness	siekte	[siktə]
to be ill	siek wees	[sik veəs]
health	gesondheid	[χesonthæjt]

runny nose (coryza)	loopneus	[loəpnøəs]
tonsillitis	keelontsteking	[keəl·ontstekiŋ]
cold (illness)	verkoue	[ferkæuə]

bronchitis	bronchitis	[bronχitis]
pneumonia	longontsteking	[loŋ·ontstekiŋ]
flu, influenza	griep	[χrip]

shortsighted (adj)	bysiende	[bajsində]
longsighted (adj)	versiende	[fersində]
strabismus (crossed eyes)	skeelheid	[skeəlhæjt]
squint-eyed (adj)	skeel	[skeəl]
cataract	katarak	[katarak]
glaucoma	gloukoom	[χlæukoəm]

stroke	beroerte	[berurtə]
heart attack	hartaanval	[hart·ānfal]
myocardial infarction	hartinfark	[hart·infark]
paralysis	verlamming	[ferlammiŋ]
to paralyse (vt)	verlam	[ferlam]

allergy	allergie	[allerχi]
asthma	asma	[asma]
diabetes	suikersiekte	[sœikər·siktə]

toothache	tandpyn	[tand·pajn]
caries	tandbederf	[tand·bederf]

diarrhoea	diarree	[diarreə]
constipation	hardlywigheid	[hardlajviχæjt]
stomach upset	maagongesteldheid	[māχ·oŋəstɛldhæjt]
food poisoning	voedselvergiftiging	[fudsəl·ferχiftəχiŋ]
to get food poisoning	voedselvergiftiging kry	[fudsəl·ferχiftəχiŋ kraj]

arthritis	artritis	[artritis]
rickets	Engelse siekte	[ɛŋəlsə siktə]
rheumatism	reumatiek	[røəmatik]
atherosclerosis	artrosklerose	[artrosklerosə]

gastritis	maagontsteking	[māχ·ontstekiŋ]
appendicitis	blindedermontsteking	[blindəderm·ontstekiŋ]
cholecystitis	galblaasontsteking	[χalblās·ontstekiŋ]

ulcer	maagsweer	[mãχsweǝr]
measles	masels	[masɛls]
rubella (German measles)	Duitse masels	[dœitsǝ masɛls]
jaundice	geelsug	[χeǝlsuχ]
hepatitis	hepatitis	[hepatitis]

schizophrenia	skisofrenie	[skisofreni]
rabies (hydrophobia)	hondsdolheid	[hondsdolhæjt]
neurosis	neurose	[nøǝrosǝ]
concussion	harsingskudding	[harsiŋ·skuddiŋ]

cancer	kanker	[kankǝr]
sclerosis	sklerose	[sklerosǝ]
multiple sclerosis	veelvuldige sklerose	[feǝlfuldiχǝ sklerosǝ]

alcoholism	alkoholisme	[alkoholismǝ]
alcoholic (n)	alkoholikus	[alkoholikus]
syphilis	sifilis	[sifilis]
AIDS	VIGS	[vigs]

tumour	tumor	[tumor]
malignant (adj)	kwaadaardig	[kwãdãrdǝχ]
benign (adj)	goedaardig	[χudãrdǝχ]

fever	koors	[koǝrs]
malaria	malaria	[malaria]
gangrene	gangreen	[χanχreǝn]
seasickness	seesiekte	[seǝ·siktǝ]
epilepsy	epilepsie	[ɛpilepsi]

epidemic	epidemie	[ɛpidemi]
typhus	tifus	[tifus]
tuberculosis	tuberkulose	[tuberkulosǝ]
cholera	cholera	[χolera]
plague (bubonic ~)	pes	[pes]

69. Symptoms. Treatments. Part 1

symptom	simptoom	[simptoǝm]
temperature	temperatuur	[temperatɪr]
high temperature (fever)	koors	[koǝrs]
pulse (heartbeat)	polsslag	[pols·slaχ]

dizziness (vertigo)	duiseligheid	[dœiseliχæjt]
hot (adj)	warm	[varm]
shivering	koue rillings	[kæʊǝ rilliŋs]
pale (e.g. ~ face)	bleek	[bleǝk]

cough	hoes	[hus]
to cough (vi)	hoes	[hus]
to sneeze (vi)	nies	[nis]
faint	floute	[flæʊtǝ]
to faint (vi)	flou word	[flæʊ vort]
bruise (hématome)	blou kol	[blæʊ kol]

bump (lump)	knop	[knop]
to bang (bump)	stamp	[stamp]
contusion (bruise)	besering	[beseriŋ]

to limp (vi)	hink	[hink]
dislocation	ontwrigting	[ontwriχtiŋ]
to dislocate (vt)	ontwrig	[ontwrəχ]
fracture	breuk	[brøək]
to have a fracture	n breuk hê	[n brøək hɛ:]

cut (e.g. paper ~)	sny	[snaj]
to cut oneself	jouself sny	[jæusɛlf snaj]
bleeding	bloeding	[bludiŋ]

| burn (injury) | brandwond | [brant·vont] |
| to get burned | jouself brand | [jæusɛlf brant] |

to prick (vt)	prik	[prik]
to prick oneself	jouself prik	[jæusɛlf prik]
to injure (vt)	seermaak	[seərmãk]
injury	besering	[beseriŋ]
wound	wond	[vont]
trauma	trauma	[trɔuma]

to be delirious	yl	[ajl]
to stutter (vi)	stotter	[stottər]
sunstroke	sonsteek	[sɔŋ·steək]

70. Symptoms. Treatments. Part 2

| pain, ache | pyn | [pajn] |
| splinter (in foot, etc.) | splinter | [splintər] |

sweat (perspiration)	sweet	[sweət]
to sweat (perspire)	sweet	[sweət]
vomiting	braak	[brãk]
convulsions	stuiptrekkings	[stœip·trɛkkiŋs]

pregnant (adj)	swanger	[swaŋər]
to be born	gebore word	[χeborə vort]
delivery, labour	geboorte	[χeboərtə]
to deliver (~ a baby)	baar	[bãr]
abortion	aborsie	[aborsi]

breathing, respiration	asemhaling	[asemhaliŋ]
in-breath (inhalation)	inaseming	[inasemiŋ]
out-breath (exhalation)	uitaseming	[œitasemiŋ]
to exhale (breathe out)	uitasem	[œitasem]
to inhale (vi)	inasem	[inasem]

disabled person	invalide	[infalidə]
cripple	kreupel	[krøəpəl]
drug addict	dwelmslaaf	[dwɛlm·slãf]
deaf (adj)	doof	[doəf]

| mute (adj) | stom | [stom] |
| deaf mute (adj) | doofstom | [doəf·stom] |

mad, insane (adj)	swaksinnig	[swaksinnəx]
madman (demented person)	kranksinnige	[kranksinnixə]
madwoman	kranksinnige	[kranksinnixə]
to go insane	kranksinnig word	[kranksinnəx vort]

gene	geen	[xeən]
immunity	immuniteit	[immunitæjt]
hereditary (adj)	erflik	[ɛrflik]
congenital (adj)	aangebore	[ānxəborə]

virus	virus	[firus]
microbe	mikrobe	[mikrobə]
bacterium	bakterie	[bakteri]
infection	infeksie	[infeksi]

71. Symptoms. Treatments. Part 3

| hospital | hospitaal | [hospitāl] |
| patient | pasiënt | [pasiɛnt] |

diagnosis	diagnose	[diaxnosə]
cure	genesing	[xenesiŋ]
medical treatment	mediese behandeling	[medisə behandəliŋ]
to get treatment	behandeling kry	[behandəliŋ kraj]
to treat (~ a patient)	behandel	[behandəl]
to nurse (look after)	versorg	[fersorx]
care (nursing ~)	versorging	[fersorxiŋ]

operation, surgery	operasie	[operasi]
to bandage (head, limb)	verbind	[ferbint]
bandaging	verband	[ferbant]

vaccination	inenting	[inɛntiŋ]
to vaccinate (vt)	inent	[inɛnt]
injection	inspuiting	[inspœitiŋ]

attack	aanval	[ānfal]
amputation	amputasie	[amputasi]
to amputate (vt)	amputeer	[amputeər]
coma	koma	[koma]
intensive care	intensiewe sorg	[intɛnsivə sorx]

to recover (~ from flu)	herstel	[herstəl]
condition (patient's ~)	kondisie	[kondisi]
consciousness	bewussyn	[bevussajn]
memory (faculty)	geheue	[xəhøə]

to pull out (tooth)	trek	[trek]
filling	vulsel	[fulsəl]
to fill (a tooth)	vul	[ful]

hypnosis	hipnose	[hipnosə]
to hypnotize (vt)	hipnotiseer	[hipnotiseər]

72. Doctors

doctor	dokter	[doktər]
nurse	verpleegster	[ferpleəχ·stər]
personal doctor	lyfarts	[lajf·arts]

dentist	tandarts	[tand·arts]
optician	oogarts	[oəχ·arts]
general practitioner	internis	[internis]
surgeon	chirurg	[ʃirurχ]

psychiatrist	psigiater	[psiχiatər]
paediatrician	kinderdokter	[kindər·doktər]
psychologist	sielkundige	[silkundiχə]
gynaecologist	ginekoloog	[χinekoloəχ]
cardiologist	kardioloog	[kardioloəχ]

73. Medicine. Drugs. Accessories

medicine, drug	medisyn	[medisajn]
remedy	geneesmiddel	[χeneəs·middəl]
to prescribe (vt)	voorskryf	[foərskrajf]
prescription	voorskrif	[foərskrif]

tablet, pill	pil	[pil]
ointment	salf	[salf]
ampoule	ampul	[ampul]
mixture, solution	mengsel	[meŋsəl]
syrup	stroop	[stroəp]
capsule	pil	[pil]
powder	poeier	[pujer]

gauze bandage	verband	[ferbant]
cotton wool	watte	[vattə]
iodine	iodium	[iodium]

plaster	pleister	[plæjstər]
eyedropper	oogdrupper	[oəχ·druppər]
thermometer	termometer	[termometər]
syringe	spuitnaald	[spœit·nãlt]

wheelchair	rolstoel	[rol·stul]
crutches	krukke	[krukkə]

painkiller	pynstiller	[pajn·stillər]
laxative	lakseermiddel	[lakseər·middəl]
spirits (ethanol)	spiritus	[spiritus]
medicinal herbs	geneeskragtige kruie	[χeneəs·kraχtiχə krœiə]
herbal (~ tea)	kruie-	[krœie-]

74. Smoking. Tobacco products

tobacco	**tabak**	[tabak]
cigarette	**sigaret**	[siχaret]
cigar	**sigaar**	[siχār]
pipe	**pyp**	[pajp]
packet (of cigarettes)	**pakkie**	[pakki]
matches	**vuurhoutjies**	[fɪrhæʊkis]
matchbox	**vuurhoutjiedosie**	[fɪrhæʊki·dosi]
lighter	**aansteker**	[āŋstekər]
ashtray	**asbak**	[asbak]
cigarette case	**sigarethouer**	[siχaret·hæʊər]
cigarette holder	**sigaretpypie**	[siχaret·pajpi]
filter (cigarette tip)	**filter**	[filtər]
to smoke (vi, vt)	**rook**	[roək]
to light a cigarette	**aansteek**	[āŋsteək]
smoking	**rook**	[roək]
smoker	**roker**	[rokər]
cigarette end	**stompie**	[stompi]
smoke, fumes	**rook**	[roək]
ash	**as**	[as]

HUMAN HABITAT

City

city, town	**stad**	[stat]
capital city	**hoofstad**	[hoəf·stat]
village	**dorp**	[dorp]
city map	**stadskaart**	[stats·kārt]
city centre	**sentrum**	[sentrum]
suburb	**voorstad**	[foərstat]
suburban (adj)	**voorstedelik**	[foərstedelik]
outskirts	**buitewyke**	[bœitəvajkə]
environs (suburbs)	**omgewing**	[omχeviŋ]
city block	**stadswyk**	[stats·wajk]
residential block (area)	**woonbuurt**	[voənbɪrt]
traffic	**verkeer**	[ferkeər]
traffic lights	**robot**	[robot]
public transport	**openbare vervoer**	[openbarə ferfur]
crossroads	**kruispunt**	[krœis·punt]
zebra crossing	**sebraoorgang**	[sebra·oərχaŋ]
pedestrian subway	**voetgangertonnel**	[futχaŋər·tonnəl]
to cross (~ the street)	**oorsteek**	[oərsteək]
pedestrian	**voetganger**	[futχaŋər]
pavement	**sypaadjie**	[saj·pādʒi]
bridge	**brug**	[bruχ]
embankment (river walk)	**wal**	[val]
fountain	**fontein**	[fontæjn]
allée (garden walkway)	**laning**	[laniŋ]
park	**park**	[park]
boulevard	**boulevard**	[bulefar]
square	**plein**	[plæjn]
avenue (wide street)	**laan**	[lān]
street	**straat**	[strāt]
side street	**systraat**	[saj·strāt]
dead end	**doodloopstraat**	[doədloəp·strāt]
house	**huis**	[hœis]
building	**gebou**	[χebæʊ]
skyscraper	**wolkekrabber**	[volkə·krabbər]
facade	**gewel**	[χevəl]
roof	**dak**	[dak]

window	venster	[fɛŋstər]
arch	arkade	[arkadə]
column	kolom	[kolom]
corner	hoek	[huk]

shop window	uitstalraam	[œitstalrām]
signboard (store sign, etc.)	reklamebord	[reklamə·bort]
poster (e.g., playbill)	plakkaat	[plakkāt]
advertising poster	reklameplakkaat	[reklamə·plakkāt]
hoarding	aanplakbord	[ānplakbort]

rubbish	vullis	[fullis]
rubbish bin	vullisbak	[fullis·bak]
to litter (vi)	rommel strooi	[rommǝl stroj]
rubbish dump	vullishoop	[fullis·hoǝp]

telephone box	telefoonhokkie	[telefoǝn·hokki]
lamppost	lamppaal	[lamp·pāl]
bench (park ~)	bank	[bank]

police officer	polisieman	[polisi·man]
police	polisie	[polisi]
beggar	bedelaar	[bedelār]
homeless (n)	daklose	[daklosǝ]

76. Urban institutions

shop	winkel	[vinkǝl]
chemist, pharmacy	apteek	[apteǝk]
optician (spectacles shop)	optisiën	[optisiɛn]
shopping centre	winkelsentrum	[vinkǝl·sentrum]
supermarket	supermark	[supermark]

bakery	bakkery	[bakkeraj]
baker	bakker	[bakkǝr]
cake shop	banketbakkery	[banket·bakkeraj]
grocery shop	kruidenierswinkel	[krœidenirs·vinkǝl]
butcher shop	slagter	[slaᵪtǝr]

| greengrocer | groentewinkel | [ᵪruntǝ·vinkǝl] |
| market | mark | [mark] |

coffee bar	koffiekroeg	[koffi·kruᵪ]
restaurant	restaurant	[restɔurant]
pub, bar	kroeg	[kruᵪ]
pizzeria	pizzeria	[pizzeria]

hairdresser	haarsalon	[hār·salon]
post office	poskantoor	[pos·kantoǝr]
dry cleaners	droogskoonmakers	[droǝᵪ·skoǝn·makers]
photo studio	fotostudio	[foto·studio]

| shoe shop | skoenwinkel | [skun·vinkǝl] |
| bookshop | boekhandel | [buk·handǝl] |

sports shop	sportwinkel	[sport·vinkəl]
clothes repair shop	klereherstelwinkel	[klerə·herstəl·vinkəl]
formal wear hire	klereverhuurwinkel	[klerə·ferhɪr·vinkəl]
video rental shop	videowinkel	[video·vinkəl]
circus	sirkus	[sirkus]
zoo	dieretuin	[dirə·tœin]
cinema	bioskoop	[bioskoəp]
museum	museum	[musøəm]
library	biblioteek	[biblioteək]
theatre	teater	[teatər]
opera (opera house)	opera	[opera]
nightclub	nagklub	[naχ·klup]
casino	kasino	[kasino]
mosque	moskee	[moskeə]
synagogue	sinagoge	[sinaχoχə]
cathedral	katedraal	[katedrãl]
temple	tempel	[tempəl]
church	kerk	[kerk]
college	kollege	[kolledʒ]
university	universiteit	[unifersitæjt]
school	skool	[skoəl]
prefecture	stadhuis	[stat·hœis]
town hall	stadhuis	[stat·hœis]
hotel	hotel	[hotəl]
bank	bank	[bank]
embassy	ambassade	[ambassadə]
travel agency	reisagentskap	[ræjs·aχentskap]
information office	inligtingskantoor	[inliχtiŋs·kantoər]
currency exchange	wisselkantoor	[vissəl·kantoər]
underground, tube	metro	[metro]
hospital	hospitaal	[hospitãl]
petrol station	petrolstasie	[petrol·stasi]
car park	parkeerterrein	[parkeər·terræjn]

77. Urban transport

bus, coach	bus	[bus]
tram	trem	[trem]
trolleybus	trembus	[trembus]
route (bus ~)	busroete	[bus·rutə]
number (e.g. bus ~)	nommer	[nommər]
to go by ...	ry per ...	[raj pər ...]
to get on (~ the bus)	inklim	[inklim]
to get off ...	uitklim ...	[œitklim ...]
stop (e.g. bus ~)	halte	[haltə]

next stop	volgende halte	[folχendə haltə]
terminus	eindpunt	[æjnd·punt]
timetable	diensrooster	[diŋs·roəstər]
to wait (vt)	wag	[vaχ]
ticket	kaartjie	[kārki]
fare	reistarief	[ræjs·tarif]
cashier (ticket seller)	kaartjieverkoper	[kārki·ferkopər]
ticket inspection	kaartjiekontrole	[kārki·kontrolə]
ticket inspector	kontroleur	[kontroløər]
to be late (for ...)	laat wees	[lāt veəs]
to miss (~ the train, etc.)	mis	[mis]
to be in a hurry	haastig wees	[hāstəχ veəs]
taxi, cab	taxi	[taksi]
taxi driver	taxibestuurder	[taksi·bestɪrdər]
by taxi	per taxi	[pər taksi]
taxi rank	taxistaanplek	[taksi·stānplek]
traffic	verkeer	[ferkeər]
traffic jam	verkeersknoop	[ferkeərs·knoəp]
rush hour	spitsuur	[spits·ɪr]
to park (vi)	parkeer	[parkeər]
to park (vt)	parkeer	[parkeər]
car park	parkeerterrein	[parkeər·terræjn]
underground, tube	metro	[metro]
station	stasie	[stasi]
to take the tube	die metro vat	[di metro fat]
train	trein	[træjn]
train station	treinstasie	[træjn·stasi]

78. Sightseeing

monument	monument	[monument]
fortress	fort	[fort]
palace	paleis	[palæjs]
castle	kasteel	[kasteəl]
tower	toring	[toriŋ]
mausoleum	mausoleum	[mɔusoløəm]
architecture	argitektuur	[arχitektɪr]
medieval (adj)	Middeleeus	[middeliʋs]
ancient (adj)	oud	[æʋt]
national (adj)	nasionaal	[naʃionāl]
famous (monument, etc.)	bekend	[bekent]
tourist	toeris	[turis]
guide (person)	gids	[χids]
excursion, sightseeing tour	uitstappie	[œitstappi]
to show (vt)	wys	[vajs]
to tell (vt)	vertel	[fertəl]

to find (vt)	vind	[fint]
to get lost (lose one's way)	verdwaal	[ferdwāl]
map (e.g. underground ~)	kaart	[kārt]
map (e.g. city ~)	kaart	[kārt]

souvenir, gift	aandenking	[āndenkiŋ]
gift shop	geskenkwinkel	[χeskɛnk·vinkəl]
to take pictures	fotografeer	[fotoχrafeər]
to have one's picture taken	jou portret laat maak	[jæʊ portret lāt māk]

79. Shopping

to buy (purchase)	koop	[koəp]
shopping	aankoop	[ānkoəp]
to go shopping	inkopies doen	[inkopis dun]
shopping	inkoop	[inkoəp]

| to be open (ab. shop) | oop wees | [oəp veəs] |
| to be closed | toe wees | [tu veəs] |

footwear, shoes	skoeisel	[skuisəl]
clothes, clothing	klere	[klerə]
cosmetics	kosmetika	[kosmetika]
food products	voedingsware	[fudiŋs·warə]
gift, present	present	[present]

| shop assistant (masc.) | verkoper | [ferkopər] |
| shop assistant (fem.) | verkoopsdame | [ferkoəps·damə] |

cash desk	kassier	[kassir]
mirror	spieël	[spiɛl]
counter (shop ~)	toonbank	[toən·bank]
fitting room	paskamer	[pas·kamər]

to try on	aanpas	[ānpas]
to fit (ab. dress, etc.)	pas	[pas]
to fancy (vt)	hou van	[hæʊ fan]

price	prys	[prajs]
price tag	pryskaartjie	[prajs·kārki]
to cost (vt)	kos	[kos]
How much?	Hoeveel?	[hufeəl?]
discount	afslag	[afslaχ]

| inexpensive (adj) | billik | [billik] |
| cheap (adj) | goedkoop | [χudkoəp] |

| expensive (adj) | duur | [dɪr] |
| It's expensive | dis duur | [dis dɪr] |

hire (n)	verhuur	[ferhɪr]
to hire (~ a dinner jacket)	verhuur	[ferhɪr]
credit (trade credit)	krediet	[kredit]
on credit (adv)	op krediet	[op kredit]

80. Money

money	geld	[χɛlt]
currency exchange	valutaruil	[faluta·rœil]
exchange rate	wisselkoers	[vissəl·kurs]
cashpoint	OTM	[o·te·em]
coin	muntstuk	[muntstuk]
dollar	dollar	[dollar]
euro	euro	[øəro]
lira	lira	[lira]
Deutschmark	Duitse mark	[dœitsə mark]
franc	frank	[frank]
pound sterling	pond sterling	[pont sterliŋ]
yen	yen	[jɛn]
debt	skuld	[skult]
debtor	skuldenaar	[skuldenãr]
to lend (money)	uitleen	[œitleən]
to borrow (vi, vt)	leen	[leən]
bank	bank	[bank]
account	rekening	[rekəniŋ]
to deposit (vt)	deponeer	[deponeər]
to withdraw (vt)	trek	[trek]
credit card	kredietkaart	[kredit·kãrt]
cash	kontant	[kontant]
cheque	tjek	[tʃek]
chequebook	tjekboek	[tʃek·buk]
wallet	beursie	[bøərsi]
purse	muntstukbeursie	[muntstuk·bøərsi]
safe	brandkas	[brant·kas]
heir	erfgenaam	[ɛrfχənãm]
inheritance	erfenis	[ɛrfenis]
fortune (wealth)	fortuin	[fortœin]
lease	huur	[hɪr]
rent (money)	huur	[hɪr]
to rent (sth from sb)	huur	[hɪr]
price	prys	[prajs]
cost	prys	[prajs]
sum	som	[som]
to spend (vt)	spandeer	[spandeər]
expenses	onkoste	[onkostə]
to economize (vi, vt)	besuinig	[besœinəχ]
economical	ekonomies	[ɛkonomis]
to pay (vi, vt)	betaal	[betãl]
payment	betaling	[betaliŋ]

change (give the ~)	wisselgeld	[vissəl·χɛlt]
tax	belasting	[belastiŋ]
fine	boete	[butə]
to fine (vt)	beboet	[bebut]

81. Post. Postal service

post office	poskantoor	[pos·kantoər]
post (letters, etc.)	pos	[pos]
postman	posbode	[pos·bodə]
opening hours	besigheidsure	[besiχæjts·urə]

letter	brief	[brif]
registered letter	geregistreerde brief	[χereχistreerdə brif]
postcard	poskaart	[pos·kārt]
telegram	telegram	[teleχram]
parcel	pakkie	[pakki]
money transfer	geldoorplasing	[χɛld·oərplasiŋ]

to receive (vt)	ontvang	[ontfaŋ]
to send (vt)	stuur	[stɪr]
sending	versending	[fersendiŋ]

address	adres	[adres]
postcode	poskode	[pos·kodə]
sender	sender	[sendər]
receiver	ontvanger	[ontfaŋər]

| name (first name) | voornaam | [foərnām] |
| surname (last name) | van | [fan] |

postage rate	postarief	[pos·tarif]
standard (adj)	standaard	[standārt]
economical (adj)	ekonomies	[ɛkonomis]

weight	gewig	[χeveχ]
to weigh (~ letters)	weeg	[veeχ]
envelope	koevert	[kufert]
postage stamp	posseël	[pos·seɛl]

Dwelling. House. Home

82. House. Dwelling

house	huis	[hœis]
at home (adv)	tuis	[tœis]
yard	werf	[verf]
fence (iron ~)	omheining	[omhæjniŋ]
brick (n)	baksteen	[baksteən]
brick (as adj)	baksteen-	[baksteən-]
stone (n)	klip	[klip]
stone (as adj)	klip-	[klip-]
concrete (n)	beton	[beton]
concrete (as adj)	beton-	[beton-]
new (new-built)	nuut	[nɪt]
old (adj)	ou	[æʊ]
decrepit (house)	vervalle	[ferfallə]
modern (adj)	moderne	[modernə]
multistorey (adj)	multiverdieping-	[multi·ferdipiŋ-]
tall (~ building)	hoë	[hoɛ]
floor, storey	verdieping	[ferdipiŋ]
single-storey (adj)	enkelverdieping	[ɛnkəl·ferdipiŋ]
ground floor	eerste verdieping	[eərstə ferdipiŋ]
top floor	boonste verdieping	[boəŋstə verdipiŋ]
roof	dak	[dak]
chimney	skoorsteen	[skoərsteən]
roof tiles	dakteëls	[dakteɛls]
tiled (adj)	geteël	[xeteɛl]
loft (attic)	solder	[soldər]
window	venster	[fɛŋstər]
glass	glas	[χlas]
window ledge	vensterbank	[fɛŋstər·bank]
shutters	luik	[lœik]
wall	muur	[mɪr]
balcony	balkon	[balkon]
downpipe	reënpyp	[reɛn·pajp]
upstairs (to be ~)	bo	[bo]
to go upstairs	boontoe gaan	[boentu χān]
to come down (the stairs)	afkom	[afkom]
to move (to new premises)	verhuis	[ferhœis]

83. House. Entrance. Lift

entrance	ingang	[inχaŋ]
stairs (stairway)	trap	[trap]
steps	treetjies	[treekis]
banisters	leuning	[løøniŋ]
lobby (hotel ~)	voorportaal	[foər·portāl]
postbox	posbus	[pos·bus]
waste bin	vullisblik	[fullis·blik]
refuse chute	vullisgeut	[fullis·χøət]
lift	hysbak	[hajsbak]
goods lift	vraghysbak	[fraχ·hajsbak]
lift cage	hysbak	[hajsbak]
to take the lift	hysbak neem	[hajsbak neəm]
flat	woonstel	[voəŋstəl]
residents (~ of a building)	bewoners	[bevoners]
neighbour (masc.)	buurman	[bɪrman]
neighbour (fem.)	buurvrou	[bɪrfræʊ]
neighbours	bure	[burə]

84. House. Doors. Locks

door	deur	[døər]
gate (vehicle ~)	hek	[hek]
handle, doorknob	deurknop	[døər·knop]
to unlock (unbolt)	oopsluit	[oəpslœit]
to open (vt)	oopmaak	[oəpmāk]
to close (vt)	sluit	[slœit]
key	sleutel	[sløətəl]
bunch (of keys)	bos	[bos]
to creak (door, etc.)	kraak	[krāk]
creak	gekraak	[χekrāk]
hinge (door ~)	skarnier	[skarnir]
doormat	deurmat	[døər·mat]
door lock	deurslot	[døər·slot]
keyhole	sleutelgat	[sløətəl·χat]
crossbar (sliding bar)	grendel	[χrendəl]
door latch	deurknip	[døər·knip]
padlock	hangslot	[haŋslot]
to ring (~ the door bell)	lui	[lœi]
ringing (sound)	gelui	[χelœi]
doorbell	deurklokkie	[døər·klokki]
doorbell button	belknoppie	[bɛl·knoppi]
knock (at the door)	klop	[klop]
to knock (vi)	klop	[klop]

code	kode	[kodə]
combination lock	kombinasieslot	[kombinasi·slot]
intercom	interkom	[interkom]
number (on the door)	nommer	[nommər]
doorplate	naambordjie	[nām·bordʒi]
peephole	loergaatjie	[lurχāki]

85. Country house

village	dorp	[dorp]
vegetable garden	groentetuin	[χruntə·tœin]
fence	heining	[hæjniŋ]
picket fence	spitspaalheining	[spitspāl·hæjniŋ]
wicket gate	tuinhekkie	[tœin·hɛkki]

granary	graanstoorplek	[χrāŋ·stoərplek]
cellar	wortelkelder	[vortəl·keldər]
shed (garden ~)	tuinhuisie	[tœin·hœisi]
water well	waterput	[vatər·put]

stove (wood-fired ~)	houtkaggel	[hæʊt·kaχχəl]
to stoke the stove	die houtkaggel stook	[di hæʊt·kaχχəl stoək]
firewood	brandhout	[brant·hæʊt]
log (firewood)	stomp	[stomp]

veranda	stoep	[stup]
deck (terrace)	dek	[dek]
stoop (front steps)	ingangstrappie	[inχaŋs·trappi]
swing (hanging seat)	swaai	[swāi]

86. Castle. Palace

castle	kasteel	[kasteəl]
palace	paleis	[palæjs]
fortress	fort	[fort]

wall (round castle)	ringmuur	[riŋ·mɪr]
tower	toring	[toriŋ]
keep, donjon	toring	[toriŋ]

portcullis	valhek	[falhek]
subterranean passage	tonnel	[tonnəl]
moat	grag	[χraχ]

chain	ketting	[kɛttiŋ]
arrow loop	skietgat	[skitχat]

magnificent (adj)	pragtig	[praχtəχ]
majestic (adj)	majestueus	[majestuøəs]

impregnable (adj)	onneembaar	[onneəmbār]
medieval (adj)	Middeleeus	[middeliʊs]

87. Flat

flat	**woonstel**	[voəŋstəl]
room	**kamer**	[kamər]
bedroom	**slaapkamer**	[slāp·kamər]
dining room	**eetkamer**	[eət·kamər]
living room	**sitkamer**	[sit·kamər]
study (home office)	**studeerkamer**	[studeər·kamər]
entry room	**ingangsportaal**	[inχaŋs·portāl]
bathroom	**badkamer**	[bad·kamər]
water closet	**toilet**	[tojlet]
ceiling	**plafon**	[plafon]
floor	**vloer**	[flur]
corner	**hoek**	[huk]

88. Flat. Cleaning

to clean (vi, vt)	**skoonmaak**	[skoənmāk]
to put away (to stow)	**bêre**	[bærə]
dust	**stof**	[stof]
dusty (adj)	**stoffig**	[stoffəχ]
to dust (vt)	**afstof**	[afstof]
vacuum cleaner	**stofsuier**	[stof·sœiər]
to vacuum (vt)	**stofsuig**	[stofsœiχ]
to sweep (vi, vt)	**vee**	[feə]
sweepings	**veegsel**	[feəχsəl]
order	**orde**	[ordə]
disorder, mess	**wanorde**	[vanordə]
mop	**mop**	[mop]
duster	**stoflap**	[stoflap]
short broom	**kort besem**	[kort besem]
dustpan	**skoppie**	[skoppi]

89. Furniture. Interior

furniture	**meubels**	[møəbɛls]
table	**tafel**	[tafel]
chair	**stoel**	[stul]
bed	**bed**	[bet]
sofa, settee	**rusbank**	[rusbank]
armchair	**gemakstoel**	[χemak·stul]
bookcase	**boekkas**	[buk·kas]
shelf	**rak**	[rak]
wardrobe	**klerekas**	[klerə·kas]
coat rack (wall-mounted ~)	**kapstok**	[kapstok]

coat stand	kapstok	[kapstok]
chest of drawers	laaikas	[lājkas]
coffee table	koffietafel	[koffi·tafəl]

mirror	spieël	[spiɛl]
carpet	mat	[mat]
small carpet	matjie	[maki]

fireplace	vuurherd	[fɪr·hert]
candle	kers	[kers]
candlestick	kandelaar	[kandelār]

drapes	gordyne	[χordajnə]
wallpaper	muurpapier	[mɪr·papir]
blinds (jalousie)	blindings	[blindiŋs]

table lamp	tafellamp	[tafel·lamp]
wall lamp (sconce)	muurlamp	[mɪr·lamp]
standard lamp	staanlamp	[stān·lamp]
chandelier	kroonlugter	[kroən·luχtər]

leg (of a chair, table)	poot	[poət]
armrest	armleuning	[arm·løəniŋ]
back (backrest)	rugleuning	[ruχ·løəniŋ]
drawer	laai	[lāi]

90. Bedding

bedclothes	beddegoed	[beddə·χut]
pillow	kussing	[kussiŋ]
pillowslip	kussingsloop	[kussiŋ·sloəp]
duvet	duvet	[dufet]
sheet	laken	[laken]
bedspread	bedsprei	[bed·spræj]

91. Kitchen

kitchen	kombuis	[kombœis]
gas	gas	[χas]
gas cooker	gasstoof	[χas·stoəf]
electric cooker	elektriese stoof	[elektrisə stoəf]
oven	oond	[oent]
microwave oven	mikrogolfoond	[mikroχolf·oent]

refrigerator	yskas	[ajs·kas]
freezer	vrieskas	[friskas]
dishwasher	skottelgoedwasser	[skottɛlχud·wassər]

mincer	vleismeul	[flæjs·møəl]
juicer	versapper	[fersappər]
toaster	broodrooster	[broəd·roəstər]
mixer	menger	[meŋər]

coffee machine	koffiemasjien	[koffi·maʃin]
coffee pot	koffiepot	[koffi·pot]
coffee grinder	koffiemeul	[koffi·møəl]

kettle	fluitketel	[flœit·ketəl]
teapot	teepot	[tee·pot]
lid	deksel	[deksəl]
tea strainer	teesiffie	[tee·siffi]

spoon	lepel	[lepəl]
teaspoon	teelepeltjie	[tee·lepəlki]
soup spoon	soplepel	[sop·lepəl]
fork	vurk	[furk]
knife	mes	[mes]

tableware (dishes)	tafelgerei	[tafel·χeræj]
plate (dinner ~)	bord	[bort]
saucer	piering	[piriŋ]

shot glass	likeurglas	[likøər·χlas]
glass (tumbler)	glas	[χlas]
cup	koppie	[koppi]

sugar bowl	suikerpot	[sœikər·pot]
salt cellar	soutvaatjie	[sæut·fāki]
pepper pot	pepervaatjie	[pepər·fāki]
butter dish	botterbakkie	[botter·bakki]

stock pot (soup pot)	soppot	[sop·pot]
frying pan (skillet)	braaipan	[brāj·pan]
ladle	opskeplepel	[opskep·lepəl]
colander	vergiet	[ferχit]
tray (serving ~)	skinkbord	[skink·bort]

bottle	bottel	[bottəl]
jar (glass)	fles	[fles]
tin (can)	blikkie	[blikki]

bottle opener	botteloopmaker	[bottəl·oəpmakər]
tin opener	blikoopmaker	[blik·oəpmakər]
corkscrew	kurktrekker	[kurk·trɛkkər]
filter	filter	[filtər]
to filter (vt)	filter	[filtər]

| waste (food ~, etc.) | vullis | [fullis] |
| waste bin (kitchen ~) | vullisbak | [fullis·bak] |

92. Bathroom

bathroom	badkamer	[bad·kamər]
water	water	[vatər]
tap	kraan	[krān]
hot water	warme water	[varmə vatər]
cold water	koue water	[kæʊə vatər]

toothpaste	**tandepasta**	[tandə·pasta]
to clean one's teeth	**tande borsel**	[tandə borsəl]
toothbrush	**tandeborsel**	[tandə·borsəl]
to shave (vi)	**skeer**	[skeər]
shaving foam	**skeerroom**	[skeər·roəm]
razor	**skeermes**	[skeər·mes]
to wash (one's hands, etc.)	**was**	[vas]
to have a bath	**bad**	[bat]
shower	**stort**	[stort]
to have a shower	**stort**	[stort]
bath	**bad**	[bat]
toilet (toilet bowl)	**toilet**	[tojlet]
sink (washbasin)	**wasbak**	[vas·bak]
soap	**seep**	[seəp]
soap dish	**seepbakkie**	[seəp·bakki]
sponge	**spons**	[spɔŋs]
shampoo	**sjampoe**	[ʃampu]
towel	**handdoek**	[handduk]
bathrobe	**badjas**	[batjas]
laundry (laundering)	**was**	[vas]
washing machine	**wasmasjien**	[vas·maʃin]
to do the laundry	**die wasgoed was**	[di vasχut vas]
washing powder	**waspoeier**	[vas·pujer]

93. Household appliances

TV, telly	**TV-stel**	[te·fe-stəl]
tape recorder	**bandspeler**	[band·spelər]
video	**videomasjien**	[video·maʃin]
radio	**radio**	[radio]
player (CD, MP3, etc.)	**speler**	[spelər]
video projector	**videoprojektor**	[video·projektor]
home cinema	**tuisfliekteater**	[tœis·flik·teatər]
DVD player	**DVD-speler**	[de·fe·de-spelər]
amplifier	**versterker**	[fersterkər]
video game console	**videokonsole**	[video·kɔŋsolə]
video camera	**videokamera**	[video·kamera]
camera (photo)	**kamera**	[kamera]
digital camera	**digitale kamera**	[diχitalə kamera]
vacuum cleaner	**stofsuier**	[stof·sœiər]
iron (e.g. steam ~)	**strykyster**	[strajk·ajstər]
ironing board	**strykplank**	[strajk·plank]
telephone	**telefoon**	[telefoən]
mobile phone	**selfoon**	[sɛlfoən]

| typewriter | tikmasjien | [tik·maʃin] |
| sewing machine | naaimasjien | [naj·maʃin] |

microphone	mikrofoon	[mikrofoən]
headphones	koptelefoon	[kop·telefoən]
remote control (TV)	afstandsbeheer	[afstands·beheər]

CD, compact disc	CD	[se·de]
cassette, tape	kasset	[kasset]
vinyl record	plaat	[plāt]

94. Repairs. Renovation

renovations	opknapwerk	[opknap·werk]
to renovate (vt)	opknap	[opknap]
to repair, to fix (vt)	herstel	[herstəl]
to put in order	aan kant maak	[ān kant māk]
to redo (do again)	oordoen	[oərdun]

paint	verf	[ferf]
to paint (~ a wall)	verf	[ferf]
house painter	skilder	[skildər]
paintbrush	verfborsel	[ferf·borsəl]

| whitewash | witkalk | [vitkalk] |
| to whitewash (vt) | wit | [vit] |

wallpaper	muurpapier	[mɪr·papir]
to wallpaper (vt)	behang	[behaŋ]
varnish	vernis	[fernis]
to varnish (vt)	vernis	[fernis]

95. Plumbing

water	water	[vatər]
hot water	warme water	[varmə vatər]
cold water	koue water	[kæʊə vatər]
tap	kraan	[krān]

drop (of water)	druppel	[druppəl]
to drip (vi)	drup	[drup]
to leak (ab. pipe)	lek	[lek]
leak (pipe ~)	lekkasie	[lɛkkasi]
puddle	poeletjie	[puləki]

pipe	pyp	[pajp]
valve (e.g., ball ~)	kraan	[krān]
to be clogged up	verstop raak	[ferstop rāk]

tools	gereedskap	[χereədskap]
adjustable spanner	skroefsleutel	[skruf·sløətəl]
to unscrew (lid, filter, etc.)	losskroef	[losskruf]

to screw (tighten)	vasskroef	[fasskruf]
to unclog (vt)	oopmaak	[oəpmāk]
plumber	loodgieter	[loədχitər]
basement	kelder	[kɛldər]
sewerage (system)	riolering	[riolerin̩]

96. Fire. Conflagration

fire (accident)	brand	[brant]
flame	vlam	[flam]
spark	vonk	[fonk]
smoke (from fire)	rook	[roək]
torch (flaming stick)	fakkel	[fakkel]
campfire	kampvuur	[kampfɪr]
petrol	petrol	[petrol]
paraffin	kerosien	[kerosin]
flammable (adj)	ontvambaar	[ontfambār]
explosive (adj)	ontplofbaar	[ontplofbār]
NO SMOKING	ROOK VERBODE	[roək ferbodə]
safety	veiligheid	[fæjliχæjt]
danger	gevaar	[χefār]
dangerous (adj)	gevaarlik	[χefārlik]
to catch fire	vlam vat	[flam fat]
explosion	ontploffing	[ontploffin̩]
to set fire	aan die brand steek	[ān di brant steek]
arsonist	brandstigter	[brant·stiχtər]
arson	brandstigting	[brant·stiχtin̩]
to blaze (vi)	brand	[brant]
to burn (be on fire)	brand	[brant]
to burn down	afbrand	[afbrant]
to call the fire brigade	die brandweer roep	[di brantveər rup]
firefighter, fireman	brandweerman	[brantveər·man]
fire engine	brandweerwa	[brantveər·wa]
fire brigade	brandweer	[brantveər]
fire engine ladder	brandweerwaleer	[brantveər·wa·leər]
fire hose	brandslang	[brant·slan̩]
fire extinguisher	brandblusser	[brant·blussər]
helmet	helmet	[hɛlmet]
siren	sirene	[sirenə]
to cry (for help)	skreeu	[skriʊ]
to call for help	hulp roep	[hulp rup]
rescuer	redder	[rɛddər]
to rescue (vt)	red	[ret]
to arrive (vi)	aankom	[ānkom]
to extinguish (vt)	blus	[blus]
water	water	[vatər]

sand	**sand**	[sant]
ruins (destruction)	**ruïnes**	[ruïnes]
to collapse (building, etc.)	**instort**	[instort]
to fall down (vi)	**val**	[fal]
to cave in (ceiling, floor)	**instort**	[instort]

| piece of debris | **brokstukke** | [brokstukkə] |
| ash | **as** | [as] |

| to suffocate (die) | **verstik** | [ferstik] |
| to be killed (perish) | **omkom** | [omkom] |

HUMAN ACTIVITIES

Job. Business. Part 1

97. Banking

bank	**bank**	[bank]
branch (of a bank)	**tak**	[tak]
consultant	**bankklerk**	[bank·klerk]
manager (director)	**bestuurder**	[bestɪrdər]
bank account	**bankrekening**	[bank·rekəniŋ]
account number	**rekeningnommer**	[rekəniŋ·nommər]
current account	**tjekrekening**	[tʃek·rekəniŋ]
deposit account	**spaarrekening**	[spãr·rekəniŋ]
to close the account	**die rekening sluit**	[di rekəniŋ slœit]
to withdraw (vt)	**trek**	[trek]
deposit	**deposito**	[deposito]
wire transfer	**telegrafiese oorplasing**	[teleχrafisə oərplasiŋ]
to wire, to transfer	**oorplaas**	[oərplãs]
sum	**som**	[som]
How much?	**Hoeveel?**	[hufeəl?]
signature	**handtekening**	[hand·tekəniŋ]
to sign (vt)	**onderteken**	[ondərtekən]
credit card	**kredietkaart**	[kredit·kãrt]
code (PIN code)	**kode**	[kodə]
credit card number	**kredietkaartnommer**	[kredit·kãrt·nommər]
cashpoint	**OTM**	[o·te·em]
cheque	**tjek**	[tʃek]
chequebook	**tjekboek**	[tʃek·buk]
loan (bank ~)	**lening**	[leniŋ]
guarantee	**waarborg**	[vãrborχ]

98. Telephone. Phone conversation

telephone	**telefoon**	[telefoən]
mobile phone	**selfoon**	[sɛlfoən]
answerphone	**antwoordmasjien**	[antwoərt·maʃin]
to call (by phone)	**bel**	[bəl]

call, ring	oproep	[oprup]
Hello!	Hallo!	[hallo!]
to ask (vt)	vra	[fra]
to answer (vi, vt)	antwoord	[antwoərt]

to hear (vt)	hoor	[hoər]
well (adv)	goed	[χut]
not well (adv)	nie goed nie	[ni χut ni]
noises (interference)	steurings	[støəriŋs]

receiver	gehoorstuk	[χehoərstuk]
to pick up (~ the phone)	optel	[optəl]
to hang up (~ the phone)	afskakel	[afskakəl]

busy (engaged)	besig	[besəχ]
to ring (ab. phone)	lui	[lœi]
telephone book	telefoongids	[telefoən·χids]

local (adj)	lokale	[lokalə]
local call	lokale oproep	[lokalə oprup]
trunk (e.g. ~ call)	langafstand	[lanχ·afstant]
trunk call	langafstand oproep	[lanχ·afstant oprup]
international (adj)	internasionale	[internaʃionalə]
international call	internasionale oproep	[internaʃionalə oprup]

99. Mobile telephone

mobile phone	selfoon	[sɛlfoən]
display	skerm	[skerm]
button	knoppie	[knoppi]
SIM card	SIMkaart	[sim·kãrt]

battery	battery	[battəraj]
to be flat (battery)	pap wees	[pap veəs]
charger	batterylaaier	[battəraj·lajer]

menu	spyskaart	[spajs·kãrt]
settings	instellings	[instɛlliŋs]
tune (melody)	wysie	[vajsi]
to select (vt)	kies	[kis]
calculator	sakrekenaar	[sakrekənãr]
voice mail	stempos	[stem·pos]
alarm clock	wekker	[vɛkkər]
contacts	kontakte	[kontaktə]

| SMS (text message) | SMS | [es·em·es] |
| subscriber | intekenaar | [intekənãr] |

100. Stationery

| ballpoint pen | bolpen | [bol·pen] |
| fountain pen | vulpen | [ful·pen] |

pencil	potlood	[potlɔət]
highlighter	merkpen	[merk·pen]
felt-tip pen	viltpen	[filt·pen]

| notepad | notaboekie | [nota·buki] |
| diary | dagboek | [daχ·buk] |

ruler	liniaal	[liniãl]
calculator	sakrekenaar	[sakrekənãr]
rubber	uitveër	[œitfeɛr]
drawing pin	duimspyker	[dœim·spajkər]
paper clip	skuifspeld	[skœif·spɛlt]

glue	gom	[χom]
stapler	krammasjien	[kram·maʃin]
hole punch	ponsmasjien	[pɔŋs·maʃin]
pencil sharpener	skerpmaker	[skerp·makər]

Job. Business. Part 2

101. Mass Media

newspaper	koerant	[kurant]
magazine	tydskrif	[tajdskrif]
press (printed media)	pers	[pers]
radio	radio	[radio]
radio station	omroep	[omrup]
television	televisie	[telefisi]
presenter, host	aanbieder	[ānbidər]
newsreader	nuusleser	[nɪslesər]
commentator	kommentator	[kommentator]
journalist	joernalis	[jurnalis]
correspondent (reporter)	korrespondent	[korrespondɛnt]
press photographer	persfotograaf	[pers·fotoχrāf]
reporter	verslaggewer	[ferslaχ·χevər]
editor	redakteur	[redaktøər]
editor-in-chief	hoofredakteur	[hoəf·redaktøər]
to subscribe (to …)	inteken op …	[intekən op …]
subscription	intekening	[intekəniŋ]
subscriber	intekenaar	[intekənār]
to read (vi, vt)	lees	[leəs]
reader	leser	[lesər]
circulation (of a newspaper)	oplaag	[oplāχ]
monthly (adj)	maandeliks	[māndəliks]
weekly (adj)	weekliks	[veəkliks]
issue (edition)	nommer	[nommər]
new (~ issue)	nuwe	[nuvə]
headline	opskrif	[opskrif]
short article	kort artikel	[kort artikəl]
column (regular article)	kolom	[kolom]
article	artikel	[artikəl]
page	bladsy	[bladsaj]
reportage, report	veslag	[feslaχ]
event (happening)	gebeurtenis	[χebøərtenis]
sensation (news)	sensasie	[sɛŋsasi]
scandal	skandaal	[skandāl]
scandalous (adj)	skandelik	[skandəlik]
great (~ scandal)	groot	[χroət]
programme (e.g. cooking ~)	program	[proχram]
interview	onderhoud	[ondərhæʊt]

| live broadcast | regstreekse uitsending | [reχstreeksə œitsendiŋ] |
| channel | kanaal | [kanãl] |

102. Agriculture

agriculture	landbou	[landbæʊ]
peasant (masc.)	boer	[bur]
peasant (fem.)	boervrou	[bur·fræʊ]
farmer	boer	[bur]

| tractor | trekker | [trɛkkər] |
| combine, harvester | stroper | [stropər] |

plough	ploeg	[pluχ]
to plough (vi, vt)	ploeg	[pluχ]
ploughland	ploegland	[pluχlant]
furrow (in field)	voor	[foər]

to sow (vi, vt)	saai	[sãi]
seeder	saaier	[sãjer]
sowing (process)	saai	[sãi]

| scythe | sens | [sɛŋs] |
| to mow, to scythe | maai | [mãi] |

| spade (tool) | graaf | [χrãf] |
| to till (vt) | omspit | [omspit] |

hoe	skoffel	[skoffəl]
to hoe, to weed	skoffel	[skoffəl]
weed (plant)	onkruid	[onkrœit]

watering can	gieter	[χitər]
to water (plants)	nat gooi	[nat χoj]
watering (act)	nat gooi	[nat χoj]

| pitchfork | gaffel | [χaffəl] |
| rake | hark | [hark] |

fertiliser	misstof	[misstof]
to fertilise (vt)	bemes	[bemes]
manure (fertiliser)	misstof	[misstof]

field	veld	[fɛlt]
meadow	weiland	[væjlant]
vegetable garden	groentetuin	[χruntə·tœin]
orchard (e.g. apple ~)	boord	[boərt]

to graze (vt)	wei	[væj]
herdsman	herder	[herdər]
pasture	weiland	[væjlant]

| cattle breeding | veeboerdery | [fee·burderaj] |
| sheep farming | skaapboerdery | [skãp·burderaj] |

plantation	**aanplanting**	[ānplantiŋ]
row (garden bed ~s)	**bedding**	[beddiŋ]
hothouse	**broeikas**	[bruikas]

drought (lack of rain)	**droogte**	[droəχtə]
dry (~ summer)	**droog**	[droəχ]

grain	**graan**	[χrān]
cereal crops	**graangewasse**	[χrān·χəwassə]
to harvest, to gather	**oes**	[us]

miller (person)	**meulenaar**	[møələnār]
mill (e.g. gristmill)	**meul**	[møəl]
to grind (grain)	**maal**	[māl]
flour	**meelblom**	[meəl·blom]
straw	**strooi**	[stroj]

103. Building. Building process

building site	**bouperseel**	[bæu·perseəl]
to build (vt)	**bou**	[bæu]
building worker	**bouwerker**	[bæu·verkər]

project	**projek**	[projek]
architect	**argitek**	[arχitek]
worker	**werker**	[verkər]

foundations (of a building)	**fondament**	[fondament]
roof	**dak**	[dak]
foundation pile	**heipaal**	[hæjpāl]
wall	**muur**	[mɪr]

reinforcing bars	**betonstaal**	[betɔŋ·stāl]
scaffolding	**steiers**	[stæjers]

concrete	**beton**	[beton]
granite	**graniet**	[χranit]
stone	**klip**	[klip]
brick	**baksteen**	[baksteən]

sand	**sand**	[sant]
cement	**sement**	[sement]
plaster (for walls)	**pleister**	[plæjstər]
to plaster (vt)	**pleister**	[plæjstər]

paint	**verf**	[ferf]
to paint (~ a wall)	**verf**	[ferf]
barrel	**drom**	[drom]

crane	**kraan**	[krān]
to lift, to hoist (vt)	**optel**	[optəl]
to lower (vt)	**laat sak**	[lāt sak]
bulldozer	**stootskraper**	[stoət·skrapər]
excavator	**graafmasjien**	[χrāf·maʃin]

scoop, bucket	**bak**	[bak]
to dig (excavate)	**grawe**	[χravə]
hard hat	**helmet**	[hɛlmet]

Professions and occupations

job	**baantjie**	[bānki]
staff (work force)	**personeel**	[personeəl]
personnel	**personeel**	[personeəl]
career	**loopbaan**	[loəpbān]
prospects (chances)	**vooruitsigte**	[foərœit·siχtə]
skills (mastery)	**meesterskap**	[meəsterskap]
selection (screening)	**seleksie**	[seleksi]
employment agency	**arbeidsburo**	[arbæjds·buro]
curriculum vitae, CV	**curriculum vitae**	[kurrikulum fitaə]
job interview	**werksonderhoud**	[werk·ondərhæʊt]
vacancy	**vakature**	[fakaturə]
salary, pay	**salaris**	[salaris]
fixed salary	**vaste salaris**	[fastə salaris]
pay, compensation	**loon**	[loən]
position (job)	**posisie**	[posisi]
duty (of an employee)	**taak**	[tāk]
range of duties	**reeks opdragte**	[reəks opdraχtə]
busy (I'm ~)	**besig**	[besəχ]
to fire (dismiss)	**afdank**	[afdank]
dismissal	**afdanking**	[afdankiŋ]
unemployment	**werkloosheid**	[verkloəshæjt]
unemployed (n)	**werkloos**	[verkloəs]
retirement	**pensioen**	[pɛnsiun]
to retire (from job)	**met pensioen gaan**	[met pɛnsiun χān]

director	**direkteur**	[direktøər]
manager (director)	**bestuurder**	[bestɪrdər]
boss	**baas**	[bās]
superior	**hoof**	[hoəf]
superiors	**hoofde**	[hoəfdə]
president	**direkteur**	[direktøər]
chairman	**voorsitter**	[foərsittər]
deputy (substitute)	**adjunk**	[adjunk]
assistant	**assistent**	[assistent]

| secretary | sekretaris | [sekretaris] |
| personal assistant | persoonlike assistent | [persoənlikə assistent] |

businessman	sakeman	[sakəman]
entrepreneur	entrepreneur	[ɛntrəprenøər]
founder	stigter	[stiχtər]
to found (vt)	stig	[stiχ]

founding member	stigter	[stiχtər]
partner	vennoot	[fɛnnoət]
shareholder	aandeelhouer	[āndeəl·hæʊər]

millionaire	miljoenêr	[miljunær]
billionaire	miljardêr	[miljardær]
owner, proprietor	eienaar	[æjenār]
landowner	grondeienaar	[χront·æjenār]

client	kliënt	[kliɛnt]
regular client	vaste kliënt	[fastə kliɛnt]
buyer (customer)	koper	[kopər]
visitor	besoeker	[besukər]

professional (n)	professioneel	[profɛssioneəl]
expert	kenner	[kɛnnər]
specialist	spesialis	[spesialis]

| banker | bankier | [bankir] |
| broker | makelaar | [makəlār] |

cashier	kassier	[kassir]
accountant	boekhouer	[bukhæʊər]
security guard	veiligheidswag	[fæjliχæjts·waχ]

investor	belegger	[beleχər]
debtor	skuldenaar	[skuldenār]
creditor	krediteur	[kreditøər]
borrower	lener	[lenər]

| importer | invoerder | [infurdər] |
| exporter | uitvoerder | [œitfurdər] |

manufacturer	produsent	[produsent]
distributor	verdeler	[ferdelər]
middleman	tussenpersoon	[tussən·persoən]

consultant	raadgewer	[rāt·χevər]
sales representative	verkoopsagent	[ferkoəps·aχent]
agent	agent	[aχent]
insurance agent	versekeringsagent	[fersəkeriŋs·aχent]

106. Service professions

| cook | kok | [kok] |
| chef (kitchen chef) | sjef | [ʃef] |

baker	bakker	[bakkər]
barman	kroegman	[kruχman]
waiter	kelner	[kɛlnər]
waitress	kelnerin	[kɛlnərin]

lawyer, barrister	advokaat	[adfokāt]
lawyer (legal expert)	prokureur	[prokurøər]
notary public	notaris	[notaris]

electrician	elektrisiën	[ɛlektrisiɛn]
plumber	loodgieter	[loədχitər]
carpenter	timmerman	[timmerman]

masseur	masseerder	[masseerdər]
masseuse	masseerster	[masseerstər]
doctor	dokter	[doktər]

taxi driver	taxibestuurder	[taksi·bestɪrdər]
driver	bestuurder	[bestɪrdər]
delivery man	koerier	[kurir]

chambermaid	kamermeisie	[kamər·mæjsi]
security guard	veiligheidswag	[fæjliχæjts·waχ]
flight attendant (fem.)	lugwaardin	[luχ·wārdin]

schoolteacher	onderwyser	[ondərwajsər]
librarian	bibliotekaris	[bibliotekaris]
translator	vertaler	[fertalər]
interpreter	tolk	[tolk]
guide	gids	[χids]

hairdresser	haarkapper	[hār·kappər]
postman	posbode	[pos·bodə]
salesman (store staff)	verkoper	[ferkopər]

gardener	tuinman	[tœin·man]
domestic servant	bediende	[bedində]
maid (female servant)	bediende	[bedində]
cleaner (cleaning lady)	skoonmaakster	[skoən·mākstər]

107. Military professions and ranks

private	soldaat	[soldāt]
sergeant	sersant	[sersant]
lieutenant	luitenant	[lœitənant]
captain	kaptein	[kaptæjn]

major	majoor	[majoər]
colonel	kolonel	[kolonəl]
general	generaal	[χenerāl]
marshal	maarskalk	[mārskalk]
admiral	admiraal	[admirāl]
military (n)	leër	[leɛr]
soldier	soldaat	[soldāt]

officer	offisier	[offisir]
commander	kommandant	[kommandant]
border guard	grenswag	[χrɛŋs·waχ]
radio operator	radio-operateur	[radio-operatøer]
scout (searcher)	verkenner	[ferkɛnnər]
pioneer (sapper)	sappeur	[sappøer]
marksman	skutter	[skuttər]
navigator	navigator	[nafiχator]

108. Officials. Priests

king	koning	[koniŋ]
queen	koningin	[koniŋin]
prince	prins	[prins]
princess	prinses	[prinsəs]
czar	tsaar	[tsār]
czarina	tsarina	[tsarina]
president	president	[president]
Secretary (minister)	minister	[ministər]
prime minister	eerste minister	[eərstə ministər]
senator	senator	[senator]
diplomat	diplomaat	[diplomāt]
consul	konsul	[kɔŋsul]
ambassador	ambassadeur	[ambassadøer]
counselor (diplomatic officer)	adviseur	[adfisøer]
official, functionary (civil servant)	amptenaar	[amptənar]
prefect	prefek	[prefek]
mayor	burgermeester	[burgər·meəstər]
judge	regter	[reχtər]
prosecutor	aanklaer	[ānklaer]
missionary	sendeling	[sendəliŋ]
monk	monnik	[monnik]
abbot	ab	[ap]
rabbi	rabbi	[rabbi]
vizier	visier	[fisir]
shah	sjah	[ʃah]
sheikh	sjeik	[ʃæjk]

109. Agricultural professions

| beekeeper | byeboer | [bajebur] |
| shepherd | herder | [herdər] |

agronomist	landboukundige	[landbæʊ·kundiχə]
cattle breeder	veeteler	[feə·telər]
veterinary surgeon	veearts	[feə·arts]

farmer	boer	[bur]
winemaker	wynmaker	[vajn·makər]
zoologist	dierkundige	[dir·kundiχə]
cowboy	cowboy	[kovboj]

110. Art professions

| actor | akteur | [aktøər] |
| actress | aktrise | [aktrisə] |

| singer (masc.) | sanger | [saŋər] |
| singer (fem.) | sangeres | [saŋəres] |

| dancer (masc.) | danser | [daŋsər] |
| dancer (fem.) | danseres | [daŋsəres] |

| performer (masc.) | verhoogkunstenaar | [ferhoəχ·kunstənãr] |
| performer (fem.) | verhoogkunstenares | [ferhoəχ·kunstənares] |

musician	musikant	[musikant]
pianist	pianis	[pianis]
guitar player	kitaarspeler	[kitãr·spelər]

conductor (orchestra ~)	dirigent	[diriχent]
composer	komponis	[komponis]
impresario	impresario	[impresario]

film director	filmregisseur	[film·reχissøər]
producer	produsent	[produsent]
scriptwriter	draaiboekskrywer	[drãjbuk·skrajvər]
critic	kritikus	[kritikus]

writer	skrywer	[skrajvər]
poet	digter	[diχtər]
sculptor	beeldhouer	[beəldhæʊər]
artist (painter)	kunstenaar	[kunstenãr]

juggler	jongleur	[jonχløər]
clown	hanswors	[haŋswors]
acrobat	akrobaat	[akrobãt]
magician	goëlaar	[χoɛlãr]

111. Various professions

doctor	dokter	[doktər]
nurse	verpleegster	[ferpleəχ·stər]
psychiatrist	psigiater	[psiχiatər]
dentist	tandarts	[tand·arts]

surgeon	chirurg	[ʃirurχ]
astronaut	astronout	[astronæʊt]
astronomer	astronoom	[astronoəm]
pilot	piloot	[piloət]

driver (of a taxi, etc.)	bestuurder	[bestɪrdər]
train driver	treindrywer	[træjn·drajvər]
mechanic	werktuigkundige	[verktœiχ·kundiχə]

miner	mynwerker	[majn·werkər]
worker	werker	[verkər]
locksmith	slotmaker	[slot·makər]
joiner (carpenter)	skrynwerker	[skrajn·werkər]
turner (lathe operator)	draaibankwerker	[drājbank·werkər]
building worker	bouwerker	[bæʊ·verkər]
welder	sweiser	[swæjsər]

professor (title)	professor	[profɛssor]
architect	argitek	[arχitek]
historian	historikus	[historikus]
scientist	wetenskaplike	[vetɛŋskaplikə]
physicist	fisikus	[fisikus]
chemist (scientist)	skeikundige	[skæjkundiχə]

archaeologist	argeoloog	[arχeoloəχ]
geologist	geoloog	[χeoloəχ]
researcher (scientist)	navorser	[naforsər]

| babysitter | babasitter | [babasittər] |
| teacher, educator | onderwyser | [ondərwajsər] |

editor	redakteur	[redaktøər]
editor-in-chief	hoofredakteur	[hoəf·redaktøər]
correspondent	korrespondent	[korrespondɛnt]
typist (fem.)	tikster	[tikstər]

designer	ontwerper	[ontwerpər]
computer expert	rekenaarkenner	[rekənār·kɛnnər]
programmer	programmeur	[proχrammøər]
engineer (designer)	ingenieur	[inχeniøər]

sailor	matroos	[matroəs]
seaman	seeman	[seəman]
rescuer	redder	[rɛddər]

firefighter	brandweerman	[brantveər·man]
police officer	polisieman	[polisi·man]
watchman	bewaker	[bevakər]
detective	speurder	[spøərdər]

customs officer	doeanebeampte	[duanə·beamptə]
bodyguard	lyfwag	[lajf·waχ]
prison officer	tronkbewaarder	[tronk·bevārdər]
inspector	inspekteur	[inspektøər]
sportsman	sportman	[sportman]
trainer, coach	breier	[bræjer]

butcher	**slagter**	[slaχtər]
cobbler (shoe repairer)	**skoenmaker**	[skun·makər]
merchant	**handelaar**	[handəlãr]
loader (person)	**laaier**	[lãjer]

| fashion designer | **modeontwerper** | [modə·ontwerpər] |
| model (fem.) | **model** | [modəl] |

112. Occupations. Social status

| schoolboy | **skoolseun** | [skoəl·søøn] |
| student (college ~) | **student** | [student] |

philosopher	**filosoof**	[filosoəf]
economist	**ekonoom**	[ɛkonoəm]
inventor	**uitvinder**	[œitfindər]

unemployed (n)	**werkloos**	[verkloəs]
retiree, pensioner	**pensioentrekker**	[pɛnsiun·trɛkkər]
spy, secret agent	**spioen**	[spiun]

prisoner	**gevangene**	[χefaŋənə]
striker	**staker**	[stakər]
bureaucrat	**burokraat**	[burokrãt]
traveller (globetrotter)	**reisiger**	[ræjsiχər]

gay, homosexual (n)	**gay**	[χaaj]
hacker	**kuberkraker**	[kubər·krakər]
hippie	**hippie**	[hippi]

bandit	**bandiet**	[bandit]
hit man, killer	**huurmoordenaar**	[hɪr·moərdenãr]
drug addict	**dwelmslaaf**	[dwɛlm·slãf]
drug dealer	**dwelmhandelaar**	[dwɛlm·handəlãr]
prostitute (fem.)	**prostituut**	[prostitɪt]
pimp	**pooier**	[pojer]

sorcerer	**towenaar**	[tovenãr]
sorceress (evil ~)	**heks**	[heks]
pirate	**piraat, seerower**	[pirãt], [seə·rovər]
slave	**slaaf**	[slãf]
samurai	**samoerai**	[samuraj]
savage (primitive)	**wilde**	[vildə]

Sports

sportsman	**sportman**	[sportman]
kind of sport	**sportsoorte**	[sport·soərtə]
basketball	**basketbal**	[basketbal]
basketball player	**basketbalspeler**	[basketbal·spelər]
baseball	**bofbal**	[bofbal]
baseball player	**bofbalspeler**	[bofbal·spelər]
football	**sokker**	[sokkər]
football player	**sokkerspeler**	[sokkər·spelər]
goalkeeper	**doelwagter**	[dul·waχtər]
ice hockey	**hokkie**	[hokki]
ice hockey player	**hokkiespeler**	[hokki·spelər]
volleyball	**vlugbal**	[fluχbal]
volleyball player	**vlugbalspeler**	[fluχbal·spelər]
boxing	**boks**	[boks]
boxer	**bokser**	[boksər]
wrestling	**stoei**	[stui]
wrestler	**stoeier**	[stujer]
karate	**karate**	[karatə]
karate fighter	**karatevegter**	[karatə·feχtər]
judo	**judo**	[judo]
judo athlete	**judoka**	[judoka]
tennis	**tennis**	[tɛnnis]
tennis player	**tennisspeler**	[tɛnnis·spelər]
swimming	**swem**	[swem]
swimmer	**swemmer**	[swemmər]
fencing	**skerm**	[skerm]
fencer	**skermer**	[skermər]
chess	**skaak**	[skāk]
chess player	**skaakspeler**	[skāk·spelər]
alpinism	**alpinisme**	[alpinismə]
alpinist	**alpinis**	[alpinis]
running	**hardloop**	[hardloəp]

runner	hardloper	[hardlopər]
athletics	atletiek	[atletik]
athlete	atleet	[atleət]

| horse riding | perdry | [perdraj] |
| horse rider | ruiter | [rœitər] |

figure skating	kunsskaats	[kuns·skāts]
figure skater (masc.)	kunsskaatser	[kuns·skātsər]
figure skater (fem.)	kunsskaatser	[kuns·skātsər]

| powerlifting | gewigoptel | [χeviχ·optəl] |
| powerlifter | gewigopteller | [χeviχ·optɛllər] |

| car racing | motorwedren | [motor·wedrən] |
| racer (driver) | renjaer | [renjaər] |

| cycling | fiets | [fits] |
| cyclist | fietser | [fitsər] |

long jump	verspring	[fer·spriŋ]
pole vaulting	polsstokspring	[polsstok·spriŋ]
jumper	springer	[spriŋər]

114. Kinds of sports. Miscellaneous

American football	sokker	[sokkər]
badminton	pluimbal	[plœimbal]
biathlon	tweekamp	[tweəkamp]
billiards	biljart	[biljart]

bobsleigh	bobslee	[bobsleə]
bodybuilding	liggaamsbou	[liχχāmsbæʊ]
water polo	waterpolo	[vatər·polo]
handball	handbal	[handbal]
golf	gholf	[golf]

rowing	roei	[rui]
scuba diving	duik	[dœik]
cross-country skiing	veldski	[fɛlt·ski]
table tennis (ping-pong)	tafeltennis	[tafel·tɛnnis]

sailing	seil	[sæjl]
rally	tydren jaag	[tajdren jāχ]
rugby	rugby	[ragbi]
snowboarding	sneeuplankry	[sniʊ·plankraj]
archery	boogskiet	[boəχ·skit]

115. Gym

| barbell | staafgewig | [stāf·χevəχ] |
| dumbbells | handgewigte | [hand·χeviχtə] |

training machine	oefenmasjien	[ufen·maʃin]
exercise bicycle	oefenfiets	[ufen·fits]
treadmill	trapmeul	[trapmøəl]

horizontal bar	rekstok	[rekstok]
parallel bars	brug	[bruχ]
vault (vaulting horse)	springperd	[spriŋ·pert]
mat (exercise ~)	oefenmat	[ufen·mat]

skipping rope	springtou	[spriŋ·tæʊ]
aerobics	aёrobiese oefeninge	[aɛrobisə ufeniŋə]
yoga	joga	[joga]

116. Sports. Miscellaneous

Olympic Games	Olimpiese Spele	[olimpisə spelə]
winner	oorwinnaar	[oərwinnãr]
to be winning	wen	[ven]
to win (vi)	wen	[ven]

| leader | leier | [læjer] |
| to lead (vi) | lei | [læj] |

first place	eerste plek	[eərstə plek]
second place	tweede plek	[tweedə plek]
third place	derde plek	[derdə plek]

medal	medalje	[medalje]
trophy	trofee	[trofeə]
prize cup (trophy)	beker	[bekər]
prize (in game)	prys	[prajs]
main prize	hoofprys	[hoəf·prajs]
record	rekord	[rekort]

| final | finale | [finalə] |
| final (adj) | finale | [finalə] |

| champion | kampioen | [kampiun] |
| championship | kampioenskap | [kampiunskap] |

stadium	stadion	[stadion]
terrace	tribune	[tribunə]
fan, supporter	ondersteuner	[ondərstøənər]
opponent, rival	teëstander	[tɛstandər]

| start (start line) | wegspringplek | [veχspriŋ·plek] |
| finish line | eindstreep | [æjnd·streəp] |

| defeat | nederlaag | [nedərlãχ] |
| to lose (not win) | verloor | [ferloər] |

referee	skeidsregter	[skæjds·reχtər]
jury (judges)	beoordelaars	[be·oərdelãrs]
score	stand	[stant]

draw	gelykspel	[χelajkspəl]
to draw (vi)	gelykop speel	[χelajkop speəl]
point	punt	[punt]
result (final score)	puntestand	[puntəstant]

| period | periode | [periodə] |
| half-time | rustyd | [rustajt] |

doping	opkikkers	[opkikkərs]
to penalise (vt)	straf	[straf]
to disqualify (vt)	diskwalifiseer	[diskwalifiseər]

apparatus	apparaat	[apparãt]
javelin	spies	[spis]
shot (metal ball)	koeël	[kuɛl]
ball (snooker, etc.)	bal	[bal]

aim (target)	doelwit	[dulwit]
target	teiken	[tæjkən]
to shoot (vi)	skiet	[skit]
accurate (~ shot)	akkuraat	[akkurãt]

trainer, coach	breier	[bræjer]
to train (sb)	afrig	[afrəχ]
to train (vi)	oefen	[ufen]
training	oefen	[ufen]

gym	gimnastieksaal	[χimnastik·sãl]
exercise (physical)	oefening	[ufeniŋ]
warm-up (athlete ~)	opwarm	[opwarm]

Education

school	**skool**	[skoəl]
headmaster	**prinsipaal**	[prinsipāl]
student (m)	**leerder**	[leərdər]
student (f)	**leerder**	[leərdər]
schoolboy	**skoolseun**	[skoəl·søən]
schoolgirl	**skooldogter**	[skoəl·doχtər]
to teach (sb)	**leer**	[leər]
to learn (language, etc.)	**leer**	[leər]
to learn by heart	**van buite leer**	[fan bœitə leər]
to learn (~ to count, etc.)	**leer**	[leər]
to be at school	**op skool wees**	[op skoəl veəs]
to go to school	**skooltoe gaan**	[skoəltu χān]
alphabet	**alfabet**	[alfabet]
subject (at school)	**vak**	[fak]
classroom	**klaskamer**	[klas·kamər]
lesson	**les**	[les]
playtime, break	**pouse**	[pæʊsə]
school bell	**skoolbel**	[skoəl·bəl]
school desk	**skoolbank**	[skoəl·bank]
blackboard	**bord**	[bort]
mark	**simbool**	[simboəl]
good mark	**goeie punt**	[χuje punt]
bad mark	**slegte punt**	[sleχtə punt]
mistake, error	**fout**	[fæʊt]
to make mistakes	**foute maak**	[fæʊtə māk]
to correct (an error)	**korrigeer**	[korriχeər]
crib	**afskryfbriefie**	[afskrajf·brifi]
homework	**huiswerk**	[hœis·werk]
exercise (in education)	**oefening**	[ufeniŋ]
to be present	**aanwesig wees**	[ānwesəχ veəs]
to be absent	**afwesig wees**	[afwesəχ veəs]
to miss school	**stokkies draai**	[stokkis drāj]
to punish (vt)	**straf**	[straf]
punishment	**straf**	[straf]
conduct (behaviour)	**gedrag**	[χedraχ]
school report	**rapport**	[rapport]

pencil	potlood	[potloət]
rubber	uitveër	[œitfeɛr]
chalk	kryt	[krajt]
pencil case	potloodsakkie	[potloət·sakki]

schoolbag	boekesak	[bukə·sak]
pen	pen	[pen]
exercise book	skryfboek	[skrajf·buk]
textbook	handboek	[hand·buk]
compasses	passer	[passər]

| to make technical drawings | tegniese tekeninge maak | [teχnisə tekənikə mãk] |
| technical drawing | tegniese tekening | [teχnisə tekəniŋ] |

poem	gedig	[χedəχ]
by heart (adv)	van buite	[fan bœitə]
to learn by heart	van buite leer	[fan bœitə leər]

school holidays	skoolvakansie	[skoəl·fakaŋsi]
to be on holiday	met vakansie wees	[met fakaŋsi veəs]
to spend holidays	jou vakansie deurbring	[jæʊ fakaŋsi døərbriŋ]

test (at school)	toets	[tuts]
essay (composition)	opstel	[opstəl]
dictation	diktee	[dikteə]

| exam (examination) | eksamen | [ɛksamen] |
| experiment (e.g., chemistry ~) | eksperiment | [ɛksperiment] |

118. College. University

academy	akademie	[akademi]
university	universiteit	[unifersitæjt]
faculty (e.g., ~ of Medicine)	fakulteit	[fakultæjt]

student (masc.)	student	[student]
student (fem.)	student	[student]
lecturer (teacher)	lektor	[lektor]

| lecture hall, room | lesingsaal | [lesiŋ·sãl] |
| graduate | gegradueerde | [χeχradueərdə] |

| diploma | sertifikaat | [sertifikãt] |
| dissertation | proefskrif | [prufskrif] |

| study (report) | navorsing | [naforsiŋ] |
| laboratory | laboratorium | [laboratorium] |

| lecture | lesing | [lesiŋ] |
| coursemate | medestudent | [medə·student] |

| scholarship, bursary | beurs | [bøərs] |
| academic degree | akademiese graad | [akademisə χrãt] |

119. Sciences. Disciplines

mathematics	wiskunde	[viskundə]
algebra	algebra	[alχebra]
geometry	meetkunde	[meetkundə]
astronomy	astronomie	[astronomi]
biology	biologie	[bioloχi]
geography	geografie	[χeoχrafi]
geology	geologie	[χeoloχi]
history	geskiedenis	[χeskidenis]
medicine	geneeskunde	[χenees·kundə]
pedagogy	pedagogie	[pedaχoχi]
law	regte	[reχtə]
physics	fisika	[fisika]
chemistry	chemie	[χemi]
philosophy	filosofie	[filosofi]
psychology	sielkunde	[silkundə]

120. Writing system. Orthography

grammar	grammatika	[χrammatika]
vocabulary	woordeskat	[voərdeskat]
phonetics	fonetika	[fonetika]
noun	selfstandige naamwoord	[sɛlfstandiχə nãmwoərt]
adjective	byvoeglike naamwoord	[bajfuχlikə nãmvoərt]
verb	werkwoord	[verk·woərt]
adverb	bijwoord	[bij·woərt]
pronoun	voornaamwoord	[foərnãm·voərt]
interjection	tussenwerpsel	[tussən·werpsəl]
preposition	voorsetsel	[foərsetsəl]
root	stam	[stam]
ending	agtervoegsel	[aχtər·fuχsəl]
prefix	voorvoegsel	[foər·fuχsəl]
syllable	lettergreep	[lɛttər·χreəp]
suffix	agtervoegsel, suffiks	[aχtər·fuχsəl], [suffiks]
stress mark	klemteken	[klem·tekən]
apostrophe	afkappingsteken	[afkappiŋs·tekən]
full stop	punt	[punt]
comma	komma	[komma]
semicolon	kommapunt	[komma·punt]
colon	dubbelpunt	[dubbəl·punt]
ellipsis	beletselteken	[beletsəl·tekən]
question mark	vraagteken	[frãχ·tekən]
exclamation mark	uitroepteken	[œitrup·tekən]

inverted commas	**aanhalingstekens**	[ānhaliŋs·tekəŋs]
in inverted commas	**tussen aanhalingstekens**	[tussən ānhaliŋs·tekəŋs]
parenthesis	**hakies**	[hakis]
in parenthesis	**tussen hakies**	[tussən hakis]
hyphen	**koppelteken**	[koppəl·tekən]
dash	**strepie**	[strepi]
space (between words)	**spasie**	[spasi]
letter	**letter**	[lɛttər]
capital letter	**hoofletter**	[hoəf·lɛttər]
vowel (n)	**klinker**	[klinkər]
consonant (n)	**konsonant**	[kɔŋsonant]
sentence	**sin**	[sin]
subject	**onderwerp**	[ondərwerp]
predicate	**predikaat**	[predikāt]
line	**reël**	[reɛl]
paragraph	**paragraaf**	[paraχrāf]
word	**woord**	[voərt]
group of words	**woordgroep**	[voərt·χrup]
expression	**uitdrukking**	[œitdrukkiŋ]
synonym	**sinoniem**	[sinonim]
antonym	**antoniem**	[antonim]
rule	**reël**	[reɛl]
exception	**uitsondering**	[œitsondəriŋ]
correct (adj)	**korrek**	[korrek]
conjugation	**vervoeging**	[ferfuχiŋ]
declension	**verbuiging**	[ferbœəχiŋ]
nominal case	**naamval**	[nāmfal]
question	**vraag**	[frāχ]
to underline (vt)	**onderstreep**	[ondərstreəp]
dotted line	**stippellyn**	[stippəl·lajn]

121. Foreign languages

language	**taal**	[tāl]
foreign (adj)	**vreemd**	[freəmt]
foreign language	**vreemde taal**	[freəmdə tāl]
to study (vt)	**studeer**	[studeər]
to learn (language, etc.)	**leer**	[leər]
to read (vi, vt)	**lees**	[leəs]
to speak (vi, vt)	**praat**	[prāt]
to understand (vt)	**verstaan**	[ferstān]
to write (vt)	**skryf**	[skrajf]
fast (adv)	**vinnig**	[finnəχ]
slowly (adv)	**stadig**	[stadəχ]

fluently (adv)	**vlot**	[flot]
rules	**reëls**	[reɛls]
grammar	**grammatika**	[χrammatika]
vocabulary	**woordeskat**	[voərdeskat]
phonetics	**fonetika**	[fonetika]
textbook	**handboek**	[hand·buk]
dictionary	**woordeboek**	[voərdə·buk]
teach-yourself book	**selfstudie boek**	[sɛlfstudi buk]
phrasebook	**taalgids**	[tāl·χids]
cassette, tape	**kasset**	[kasset]
videotape	**videoband**	[video·bant]
CD, compact disc	**CD**	[se·de]
DVD	**DVD**	[de·fe·de]
alphabet	**alfabet**	[alfabet]
to spell (vt)	**spel**	[spel]
pronunciation	**uitspraak**	[œitsprāk]
accent	**aksent**	[aksent]
word	**woord**	[voərt]
meaning	**betekenis**	[betekənis]
course (e.g. a French ~)	**kursus**	[kursus]
to sign up	**inskryf**	[inskrajf]
teacher	**onderwyser**	[ondərwajsər]
translation (process)	**vertaling**	[fertaliŋ]
translation (text, etc.)	**vertaling**	[fertaliŋ]
translator	**vertaler**	[fertalər]
interpreter	**tolk**	[tolk]
polyglot	**poliglot**	[poliχlot]
memory	**geheue**	[χəhøə]

122. Fairy tale characters

Father Christmas	**Kersvader**	[kers·fadər]
Cinderella	**Assepoester**	[assepustər]
mermaid	**meermin**	[meərmin]
Neptune	**Neptunus**	[neptunus]
magician, wizard	**towenaar**	[tovenār]
fairy	**feetjie**	[feəki]
magic (adj)	**magies**	[maχis]
magic wand	**towerstaf**	[tovər·staf]
fairy tale	**sprokie**	[sproki]
miracle	**wonderwerk**	[vondərwerk]
dwarf	**dwerg**	[dwerχ]
to turn into ...	**verander in ...**	[ferandər in ...]
ghost	**gees**	[χeəs]
phantom	**spook**	[spoək]

monster	monster	[mɔŋstər]
dragon	draak	[drãk]
giant	reus	[røəs]

123. Zodiac Signs

Aries	Ram	[ram]
Taurus	Stier	[stir]
Gemini	Tweelinge	[tweəliŋə]
Cancer	Kreef	[kreəf]
Leo	Leeu	[liʊ]
Virgo	Maagd	[mãχt]

Libra	Weegskaal	[veəχskãl]
Scorpio	Skerpioen	[skerpiun]
Sagittarius	Boogskutter	[boəχskuttər]
Capricorn	Steenbok	[steənbok]
Aquarius	Waterman	[vatərman]
Pisces	Visse	[fissə]

character	karakter	[karaktər]
character traits	karaktertrekke	[karaktər·trɛkkə]
behaviour	gedrag	[χedraχ]
to tell fortunes	waarsê	[vãrsɛ:]
fortune-teller	waarsêer	[vãrsɛər]
horoscope	horoskoop	[horoskoəp]

Arts

theatre	teater	[teatər]
opera	opera	[opera]
operetta	operette	[opercttə]
ballet	ballet	[ballet]

theatre poster	plakkaat	[plakkãt]
theatre company	teatergeselskap	[teatər·xesɛlskap]
tour	toer	[tur]
to be on tour	op toer wees	[op tur veəs]
to rehearse (vi, vt)	repeteer	[repeteər]
rehearsal	repetisie	[repetisi]
repertoire	repertoire	[repertuarə]

performance	voorstelling	[foərstɛlliŋ]
theatrical show	opvoering	[opfuriŋ]
play	toneelstuk	[toneəl·stuk]

ticket	kaartjie	[kãrki]
booking office	loket	[lokət]
lobby, foyer	voorportaal	[foər·portãl]
coat check (cloakroom)	bewaarkamer	[bevãr·kamər]
cloakroom ticket	bewaarkamerkaartjie	[bevãr·kamər·kãrki]
binoculars	verkyker	[ferkajkər]
usher	plekaanwyser	[plek·ãnwajsər]

stalls (orchestra seats)	stalles	[stalles]
balcony	balkon	[balkon]
dress circle	eerste balkon	[eərstə balkon]
box	losie	[losi]
row	ry	[raj]
seat	sitplek	[sitplek]

audience	gehoor	[xehoər]
spectator	toehoorders	[tuhoərders]
to clap (vi, vt)	klap	[klap]
applause	applous	[applæʊs]
ovation	toejuiging	[tujœəχiŋ]

stage	verhoog	[ferhoəχ]
curtain	gordyn	[χordajn]
scenery	dekor	[dekor]
backstage	agter die verhoog	[aχtər di ferhoəχ]

scene (e.g. the last ~)	toneel	[toneəl]
act	bedryf	[bedrajf]
interval	pouse	[pæʊsə]

125. Cinema

actor	**akteur**	[aktøər]
actress	**aktrise**	[aktrisə]
cinema (industry)	**filmbedryf**	[film·bedrajf]
film	**fliek**	[flik]
episode	**episode**	[ɛpisodə]
detective film	**speurfliek**	[spøər·flik]
action film	**aksiefliek**	[aksi·flik]
adventure film	**avontuurfliek**	[afontɪr·flik]
science fiction film	**wetenskapfiksiefilm**	[vetɛŋskapfiksi·film]
horror film	**gruwelfliek**	[χruvɛl·flik]
comedy film	**komedie**	[komedi]
melodrama	**melodrama**	[melodrama]
drama	**drama**	[drama]
fictional film	**rolprent**	[rolprent]
documentary	**dokumentêre rolprent**	[dokumentɛrə rolprent]
cartoon	**tekenfilm**	[tekən·film]
silent films	**stilprent**	[stil·prent]
role (part)	**rol**	[rol]
leading role	**hoofrol**	[hoəf·rol]
to play (vi, vt)	**speel**	[speəl]
film star	**filmster**	[film·stər]
well-known (adj)	**bekend**	[bekent]
famous (adj)	**beroemd**	[berumt]
popular (adj)	**gewild**	[χevilt]
script (screenplay)	**draaiboek**	[drãjbuk]
scriptwriter	**draaiboekskrywer**	[drãjbuk·skrajvər]
film director	**filmregisseur**	[film·reχissøər]
producer	**produsent**	[produsent]
assistant	**assistent**	[assistent]
cameraman	**kameraman**	[kameraman]
stuntman	**waaghals**	[vãχhals]
double (body double)	**dubbel**	[dubbəl]
audition, screen test	**filmtoets**	[film·tuts]
shooting	**skiet**	[skit]
film crew	**filmspan**	[film·span]
film set	**rolprentstel**	[rolprent·stəl]
camera	**kamera**	[kamera]
cinema	**bioskoop**	[bioskoəp]
screen (e.g. big ~)	**skerm**	[skerm]
soundtrack	**klankbaan**	[klank·bān]
special effects	**spesiale effekte**	[spesialə ɛffektə]
subtitles	**onderskrif**	[ondərskrif]
credits	**erkenning**	[ɛrkɛnniŋ]
translation	**vertaling**	[fertaliŋ]

126. Painting

art	kuns	[kuns]
fine arts	skone kunste	[skonə kunstə]
art gallery	kunsgalery	[kuns·ɣalɛraj]
art exhibition	kunsuitstalling	[kuns·œitstalliŋ]
painting (art)	skildery	[skilderaj]
graphic art	grafiese kuns	[ɣrafisə kuns]
abstract art	abstrakte kuns	[abstraktə kuns]
impressionism	impressionisme	[imprɛssionismə]
picture (painting)	skildery	[skilderaj]
drawing	tekening	[tekəniŋ]
poster	plakkaat	[plakkāt]
illustration (picture)	illustrasie	[illustrasi]
miniature	miniatuur	[miniatɪr]
copy (of painting, etc.)	kopie	[kopi]
reproduction	reproduksie	[reproduksi]
mosaic	mosaiek	[mosajek]
stained glass window	gebrandskilderde venster	[ɣebrandskilderdə fɛnstər]
fresco	fresko	[fresko]
engraving	gravure	[ɣrafurə]
bust (sculpture)	borsbeeld	[borsbeəlt]
sculpture	beeldhouwerk	[beəldhæuverk]
statue	standbeeld	[standbeəlt]
plaster of Paris	gips	[ɣips]
plaster (as adj)	gips-	[ɣips-]
portrait	portret	[portret]
self-portrait	selfportret	[sɛlf·portret]
landscape painting	landskap	[landskap]
still life	stillewe	[stillevə]
caricature	karikatuur	[karikatɪr]
sketch	skets	[skets]
paint	verf	[ferf]
watercolor paint	waterverf	[vatər·ferf]
oil (paint)	olieverf	[oli·ferf]
pencil	potlood	[potloət]
Indian ink	Indiese ink	[indisə ink]
charcoal	houtskool	[hæuts·koəl]
to draw (vi, vt)	teken	[tekən]
to paint (vi, vt)	skilder	[skildər]
to pose (vi)	poseer	[poseər]
artist's model (masc.)	naakmodel	[nākmodəl]
artist's model (fem.)	naakmodel	[nākmodəl]
artist (painter)	kunstenaar	[kunstenār]
work of art	kunswerk	[kuns·werk]

| masterpiece | meesterstuk | [meəstər·stuk] |
| studio (artist's workroom) | studio | [studio] |

canvas (cloth)	doek	[duk]
easel	skildersesel	[skilders·esəl]
palette	palet	[palet]

frame (picture ~, etc.)	raam	[rãm]
restoration	restourasie	[restæʊrasi]
to restore (vt)	restoureer	[restæʊreər]

127. Literature & Poetry

literature	literatuur	[literatɪr]
author (writer)	skrywer	[skrajvər]
pseudonym	skuilnaam	[skœil·nãm]

book	boek	[buk]
volume	deel	[deəl]
table of contents	inhoudsopgawe	[inhæʊds·opχavə]
page	bladsy	[bladsaj]
main character	hoofkarakter	[hoəf·karaktər]
autograph	outograaf	[æʊtoχrãf]

short story	kortverhaal	[kort·ferhãl]
story (novella)	novelle	[nofɛllə]
novel	roman	[roman]
work (writing)	werk	[verk]
fable	fabel	[fabəl]
detective novel	speurroman	[spøər·roman]

poem (verse)	gedig	[χedəχ]
poetry	digkuns	[diχkuns]
poem (epic, ballad)	epos	[ɛpos]
poet	digter	[diχtər]

fiction	fiksie	[fiksi]
science fiction	wetenskapsfiksie	[vetɛŋskaps·fiksi]
adventures	avonture	[afonturə]
educational literature	opvoedkundige literatuur	[opfutkundiχə literatɪr]
children's literature	kinderliteratuur	[kindər·literatɪr]

128. Circus

circus	sirkus	[sirkus]
travelling circus	rondreisende sirkus	[rondræjsendə sirkus]
programme	program	[proχram]
performance	voorstelling	[foərstɛlliŋ]

act (circus ~)	nommer	[nommər]
circus ring	sirkusring	[sirkus·riŋ]
pantomime (act)	pantomime	[pantomimə]

clown	hanswors	[haŋswors]
acrobat	akrobaat	[akrobãt]
acrobatics	akrobatiek	[akrobatik]
gymnast	gimnas	[χimnas]
acrobatic gymnastics	gimnastiek	[χimnastik]
somersault	salto	[salto]

strongman	atleet	[atleət]
tamer (e.g., lion ~)	temmer	[tɛmmər]
rider (circus horse ~)	ruiter	[rœitər]
assistant	assistent	[assistent]

stunt	waaghalsige toertjie	[vãχhalsiχə turki]
magic trick	goëltoertjie	[χoɛl·turki]
conjurer, magician	goëlaar	[χoɛlãr]

juggler	jongleur	[jonχløər]
to juggle (vi, vt)	jongleer	[jonχleər]
animal trainer	dresseerder	[drɛsseər·dər]
animal training	dressering	[drɛsseriŋ]
to train (animals)	afrig	[afrəχ]

129. Music. Pop music

music	musiek	[musik]
musician	musikant	[musikant]
musical instrument	musiekinstrument	[musik·instrument]
to play ...	speel ...	[speəl ...]

guitar	kitaar	[kitãr]
violin	viool	[fioəl]
cello	tjello	[tʃello]
double bass	kontrabas	[kontrabas]
harp	harp	[harp]

piano	piano	[piano]
grand piano	vleuelklavier	[fløɛl·klafir]
organ	orrel	[orrəl]

wind instruments	blaasinstrumente	[blãs·instrumentə]
oboe	hobo	[hobo]
saxophone	saksofoon	[saksofoən]
clarinet	klarinet	[klarinet]
flute	dwarsfluit	[dwars·flœit]
trumpet	trompet	[trompet]

| accordion | trekklavier | [trɛkklafir] |
| drum | trommel | [tromməl] |

duo	duet	[duet]
trio	trio	[trio]
quartet	kwartet	[kwartet]
choir	koor	[koər]
orchestra	orkes	[orkes]

pop music	popmusiek	[pop·musik]
rock music	rockmusiek	[rok·musik]
rock group	rockgroep	[rok·xrup]
jazz	jazz	[jazz]

| idol | held | [hɛlt] |
| admirer, fan | bewonderaar | [bevondərãr] |

concert	konsert	[kɔŋsert]
symphony	simfonie	[simfoni]
composition	komposisie	[komposisi]
to compose (write)	komponeer	[komponeər]

singing (n)	sang	[saŋ]
song	lied	[lit]
tune (melody)	wysie	[vajsi]
rhythm	ritme	[ritmə]
blues	blues	[blues]

sheet music	bladmusiek	[blad·musik]
baton	dirigeerstok	[dirixeər·stok]
bow	strykstok	[strajk·stok]
string	snaar	[snãr]
case (e.g. guitar ~)	houer	[hæʊər]

Rest. Entertainment. Travel

130. Trip. Travel

tourism, travel	**toerisme**	[turismə]
tourist	**toeris**	[turis]
trip, voyage	**reis**	[ræjs]
adventure	**avontuur**	[afontɪr]
trip, journey	**reis**	[ræjs]
holiday	**vakansie**	[fakaŋsi]
to be on holiday	**met vakansie wees**	[met fakaŋsi veəs]
rest	**rus**	[rus]
train	**trein**	[træjn]
by train	**per trein**	[pər træjn]
aeroplane	**vliegtuig**	[fliχtœiχ]
by aeroplane	**per vliegtuig**	[pər fliχtœiχ]
by car	**per motor**	[pər motor]
by ship	**per skip**	[pər skip]
luggage	**bagasie**	[baχasi]
suitcase	**tas**	[tas]
luggage trolley	**bagasiekarretjie**	[baχasi·karrəki]
passport	**paspoort**	[paspoərt]
visa	**visum**	[fisum]
ticket	**kaartjie**	[kārki]
air ticket	**lugkaartjie**	[luχ·kārki]
guidebook	**reisgids**	[ræjsχids]
map (tourist ~)	**kaart**	[kārt]
area (rural ~)	**gebied**	[χebit]
place, site	**plek**	[plek]
exotica (n)	**eksotiese dinge**	[ɛksotisə diŋə]
exotic (adj)	**eksoties**	[ɛksotis]
amazing (adj)	**verbasend**	[ferbasent]
group	**groep**	[χrup]
excursion, sightseeing tour	**uitstappie**	[œitstappi]
guide (person)	**gids**	[χids]

131. Hotel

hotel	**hotel**	[hotəl]
motel	**motel**	[motəl]
three-star (~ hotel)	**drie-ster**	[dri-stər]

five-star	**vyf-ster**	[fajf-stər]
to stay (in a hotel, etc.)	**oornag**	[oərnaχ]
room	**kamer**	[kamər]
single room	**enkelkamer**	[ɛnkəl·kamər]
double room	**dubbelkamer**	[dubbəl·kamər]
half board	**met aandete, bed en ontbyt**	[met ãndetə], [bet en ontbajt]
full board	**volle losies**	[follə losis]
with bath	**met bad**	[met bat]
with shower	**met stortbad**	[met stort·bat]
satellite television	**satelliet-TV**	[satɛllit-te·fe]
air-conditioner	**lugversorger**	[luχfersorχər]
towel	**handdoek**	[handduk]
key	**sleutel**	[sløətəl]
administrator	**bestuurder**	[bestɪrdər]
chambermaid	**kamermeisie**	[kamər·mæjsi]
porter	**hoteljoggie**	[hotəl·joχi]
doorman	**portier**	[portir]
restaurant	**restaurant**	[restɔurant]
pub, bar	**kroeg**	[kruχ]
breakfast	**ontbyt**	[ontbajt]
dinner	**aandete**	[ãndetə]
buffet	**buffetete**	[buffetetə]
lobby	**voorportaal**	[foər·portãl]
lift	**hysbak**	[hajsbak]
DO NOT DISTURB	**MOENIE STEUR NIE**	[muni støər ni]
NO SMOKING	**ROOK VERBODE**	[roɛk ferbodə]

132. Books. Reading

book	**boek**	[buk]
author	**outeur**	[æʊtøər]
writer	**skrywer**	[skrajvər]
to write (~ a book)	**skryf**	[skrajf]
reader	**leser**	[lesər]
to read (vi, vt)	**lees**	[leəs]
reading (activity)	**lees**	[leəs]
silently (to oneself)	**stil**	[stil]
aloud (adv)	**hardop**	[hardop]
to publish (vt)	**uitgee**	[œitχeə]
publishing (process)	**uitgee**	[œitχeə]
publisher	**uitgewer**	[œitχevər]
publishing house	**uitgewery**	[œitχeveraj]
to come out (be released)	**verskyn**	[ferskajn]
release (of a book)	**verskyn**	[ferskajn]

print run	**oplaag**	[oplāχ]
bookshop	**boekhandel**	[buk·handəl]
library	**biblioteek**	[biblioteək]
story (novella)	**novelle**	[nofɛllə]
short story	**kortverhaal**	[kort·ferhāl]
novel	**roman**	[roman]
detective novel	**speurroman**	[spøər·roman]
memoirs	**memoires**	[memuares]
legend	**legende**	[leχendə]
myth	**mite**	[mitə]
poetry, poems	**poësie**	[poɛsi]
autobiography	**outobiografie**	[æutobioχrafi]
selected works	**bloemlesing**	[blumlesiŋ]
science fiction	**wetenskapsfiksie**	[vetɛŋskaps·fiksi]
title	**titel**	[titel]
introduction	**inleiding**	[inlæjdiŋ]
title page	**titelblad**	[titel·blat]
chapter	**hoofstuk**	[hoəfstuk]
extract	**fragment**	[fraχment]
episode	**episode**	[ɛpisodə]
plot (storyline)	**plot**	[plot]
contents	**inhoud**	[inhæut]
table of contents	**inhoudsopgawe**	[inhæuds·opχavə]
main character	**hoofkarakter**	[hoəf·karaktər]
volume	**deel**	[deəl]
cover	**omslag**	[omslaχ]
binding	**band**	[bant]
bookmark	**bladwyser**	[blat·vajsər]
page	**bladsy**	[bladsaj]
to page through	**deurblaai**	[døərblāi]
margins	**marges**	[marχəs]
annotation (marginal note, etc.)	**annotasie**	[annotasi]
footnote	**voetnota**	[fut·nota]
text	**teks**	[teks]
type, fount	**lettertipe**	[lɛttər·tipə]
misprint, typo	**drukfout**	[druk·fæut]
translation	**vertaling**	[fertaliŋ]
to translate (vt)	**vertaal**	[fertāl]
original (n)	**oorspronklike**	[oərspronklikə]
famous (adj)	**beroemd**	[berumt]
unknown (not famous)	**onbekend**	[onbekent]
interesting (adj)	**interessante**	[interessantə]
bestseller	**blitsverkoper**	[blits·ferkopər]
dictionary	**woordeboek**	[voərdə·buk]

| textbook | handboek | [hand·buk] |
| encyclopedia | ensiklopedie | [ɛŋsiklopedi] |

133. Hunting. Fishing

hunting	jag	[jaχ]
to hunt (vi, vt)	jag	[jaχ]
hunter	jagter	[jaχtər]

to shoot (vi)	skiet	[skit]
rifle	geweer	[χeveər]
bullet (shell)	patroon	[patroən]
shot (lead balls)	hael	[haəl]

steel trap	slagyster	[slaχ·ajstər]
snare (for birds, etc.)	valstrik	[falstrik]
to fall into the steel trap	in die valstrik trap	[in di falstrik trap]
to lay a steel trap	n valstrik lê	[ə falstrik lɛ:]
poacher	wildstroper	[vilt·stropər]
game (in hunting)	wild	[vilt]
hound dog	jaghond	[jaχ·hont]
safari	safari	[safari]
mounted animal	opgestopte dier	[opχestoptə dir]

fisherman	visterman	[fisterman]
fishing (angling)	vis vang	[fis faŋ]
to fish (vi)	vis vang	[fis faŋ]
fishing rod	visstok	[fis·stok]
fishing line	vislyn	[fis·lajn]
hook	vishoek	[fis·huk]
float	vlotter	[flottər]
bait	aas	[ās]

to cast a line	lyngooi	[lajnχoj]
to bite (ab. fish)	byt	[bajt]
catch (of fish)	vang	[faŋ]
ice-hole	gat in die ys	[χat in di ajs]

fishing net	visnet	[fis·net]
boat	boot	[boət]
to cast[throw] the net	die net gooi	[di net χoj]
to haul the net in	die net intrek	[di net intrek]
to fall into the net	in die net val	[in di net fal]

whaler (person)	walvisvanger	[valfis·vaŋər]
whaleboat	walvisboot	[valfis·boət]
harpoon	harpoen	[harpun]

134. Games. Billiards

| billiards | biljart | [biljart] |
| billiard room, hall | biljartkamer | [biljart·kamər] |

ball (snooker, etc.)	bal	[bal]
cue	biljartstok	[biljart·stok]
pocket	sakkie	[sakki]

135. Games. Playing cards

diamonds	diamante	[diamantə]
spades	skoppens	[skoppɛns]
hearts	harte	[hartə]
clubs	klawers	[klavərs]

ace	aas	[ãs]
king	koning	[koniŋ]
queen	dame	[damə]
jack, knave	boer	[bur]

playing card	speelkaart	[speəl·kãrt]
cards	kaarte	[kãrtə]
trump	troefkaart	[truf·kãrt]
pack of cards	pak kaarte	[pak kãrtə]

point	punt	[punt]
to deal (vi, vt)	uitdeel	[œitdeəl]
to shuffle (cards)	skommel	[skomməl]
lead, turn (n)	beurt	[bøərt]
cardsharp	valsspeler	[fals·spelər]

136. Rest. Games. Miscellaneous

to stroll (vi, vt)	wandel	[vandəl]
stroll (leisurely walk)	wandeling	[vandəliŋ]
car ride	motorrit	[motor·rit]
adventure	avontuur	[afontɪr]
picnic	piekniek	[piknik]

game (chess, etc.)	spel	[spel]
player	speler	[spelər]
game (one ~ of chess)	spel	[spel]

collector (e.g. philatelist)	versamelaar	[fersamelãr]
to collect (stamps, etc.)	versamel	[fersaməl]
collection	versameling	[fersaməliŋ]

crossword puzzle	blokkiesraaisel	[blokkis·rãisəl]
racecourse (hippodrome)	perderesiesbaan	[perdə·resisbãn]
disco (discotheque)	disko	[disko]

| sauna | sauna | [sɔuna] |
| lottery | lotery | [loteraj] |

| camping trip | kampeeruitstappie | [kampeər·ajtstappi] |
| camp | kamp | [kamp] |

tent (for camping)	**tent**	[tɛnt]
compass	**kompas**	[kompas]
camper	**kampeerder**	[kampeərdər]

to watch (film, etc.)	**kyk**	[kajk]
viewer	**kyker**	[kajkər]
TV show (TV program)	**TV-program**	[te·fe-proχram]

137. Photography

| camera (photo) | **kamera** | [kamera] |
| photo, picture | **foto** | [foto] |

photographer	**fotograaf**	[fotoχrãf]
photo studio	**fotostudio**	[foto·studio]
photo album	**fotoalbum**	[foto·album]

camera lens	**kameralens**	[kamera·lɛŋs]
telephoto lens	**telefotolens**	[telefoto·lɛŋs]
filter	**filter**	[filtər]
lens	**lens**	[lɛŋs]
optics (high-quality ~)	**optiek**	[optik]
diaphragm (aperture)	**diafragma**	[diafraχma]
exposure time (shutter speed)	**beligtingstyd**	[beliχtiŋs·tajt]
viewfinder	**soeker**	[sukər]

digital camera	**digitale kamera**	[diχitalə kamera]
tripod	**driepoot**	[dripoət]
flash	**flits**	[flits]
to photograph (vt)	**fotografeer**	[fotoχrafeər]
to take pictures	**fotografeer**	[fotoχrafeər]
to have one's picture taken	**jou portret laat maak**	[jæʊ portret lãt mãk]

focus	**fokus**	[fokus]
to focus	**fokus**	[fokus]
sharp, in focus (adj)	**skerp**	[skerp]
sharpness	**skerpheid**	[skerphæjt]

| contrast | **kontras** | [kontras] |
| contrast (as adj) | **kontrasryk** | [kontrasrajk] |

picture (photo)	**kiekie**	[kiki]
negative (n)	**negatief**	[neχatif]
film (a roll of ~)	**rolfilm**	[rolfilm]
frame (still)	**raampie**	[rãmpi]
to print (photos)	**druk**	[druk]

138. Beach. Swimming

| beach | **strand** | [strant] |
| sand | **sand** | [sant] |

deserted (beach)	verlate	[ferlatə]
suntan	sonbruin kleur	[sonbrœin kløər]
to get a tan	bruinbrand	[brœinbrant]
tanned (adj)	bruingebrand	[brœiŋəbrant]
sunscreen	sonskermroom	[sɔŋ·skerm·roəm]
bikini	bikini	[bikini]
swimsuit, bikini	baaikostuum	[bāj·kostɪm]
swim trunks	baaibroek	[bāj·bruk]
swimming pool	swembad	[swem·bat]
to swim (vi)	swem	[swem]
shower	stort	[stort]
to change (one's clothes)	verklee	[ferkleə]
towel	handdoek	[handduk]
boat	boot	[boət]
motorboat	motorboot	[motor·boət]
water ski	waterski	[vatər·ski]
pedalo	waterfiets	[vatər·fits]
surfing	branderplankry	[brandərplank·raj]
surfer	branderplankryer	[brandərplank·rajer]
scuba set	duiklong	[dœiklɔŋ]
flippers (swim fins)	paddavoet	[padda·fut]
mask (diving ~)	duikmasker	[dœik·maskər]
diver	duiker	[dœikər]
to dive (vi)	duik	[dœik]
underwater (adv)	onder water	[ondər vatər]
beach umbrella	strandsambreel	[strand·sambreəl]
beach chair (sun lounger)	strandstoel	[strand·stul]
sunglasses	sonbril	[son·bril]
air mattress	opblaasmatras	[opblās·matras]
to play (amuse oneself)	speel	[speəl]
to go for a swim	gaan swem	[xān swem]
beach ball	strandbal	[strand·bal]
to inflate (vt)	opblaas	[opblās]
inflatable, air (adj)	opblaas-	[opblās-]
wave	golf	[xolf]
buoy (line of ~s)	boei	[bui]
to drown (ab. person)	verdrink	[ferdrink]
to save, to rescue	red	[ret]
life jacket	reddingsbaadjie	[rɛddiŋs·bādʒi]
to observe, to watch	dophou	[dophæʊ]
lifeguard	lewensredder	[levɛŋs·rɛddər]

TECHNICAL EQUIPMENT. TRANSPORT

Technical equipment

139. Computer

computer	**rekenaar**	[rekənār]
notebook, laptop	**skootrekenaar**	[skoət·rekənār]
to turn on	**aanskakel**	[ānskakəl]
to turn off	**afskakel**	[afskakəl]
keyboard	**toetsbord**	[tuts·bort]
key	**toets**	[tuts]
mouse	**muis**	[mœis]
mouse mat	**muismatjie**	[mœis·maki]
button	**knop**	[knop]
cursor	**loper**	[lopər]
monitor	**monitor**	[monitor]
screen	**skerm**	[skerm]
hard disk	**harde skyf**	[hardə skajf]
hard disk capacity	**harde skyf se vermoë**	[hardə skajf sə fermoɛ]
memory	**geheue**	[χəhøə]
random access memory	**RAM-geheue**	[ram-χehøəə]
file	**lêer**	[lɛər]
folder	**gids**	[χids]
to open (vt)	**oopmaak**	[oəpmāk]
to close (vt)	**sluit**	[slœit]
to save (vt)	**bewaar**	[bevār]
to delete (vt)	**uitvee**	[œitfeə]
to copy (vt)	**kopieer**	[kopir]
to sort (vt)	**sorteer**	[sorteər]
to transfer (copy)	**oorplaas**	[oərplās]
programme	**program**	[proχram]
software	**sagteware**	[saχtevarə]
programmer	**programmeur**	[proχrammøər]
to program (vt)	**programmeer**	[proχrammeər]
hacker	**kuberkraker**	[kubər·krakər]
password	**wagwoord**	[vaχ·woərt]
virus	**virus**	[firus]
to find, to detect	**opspoor**	[opspoər]
byte	**greep**	[χreəp]

megabyte	megagreep	[meχaχreəp]
data	data	[data]
database	databasis	[data·basis]

cable (USB, etc.)	kabel	[kabəl]
to disconnect (vt)	ontkoppel	[ontkoppəl]
to connect (sth to sth)	konnekteer	[konnekteər]

140. Internet. E-mail

Internet	internet	[internet]
browser	webblaaier	[veb·blājer]
search engine	soekenjin	[suk·ɛnʤin]
provider	verskaffer	[ferskaffər]

webmaster	webmeester	[veb·meəstər]
website	webwerf	[veb·werf]
web page	webblad	[veb·blat]

| address (e-mail ~) | adres | [adres] |
| address book | adresboek | [adres·buk] |

postbox	posbus	[pos·bus]
post	pos	[pos]
full (adj)	vol	[fol]

message	boodskap	[boədskap]
incoming messages	inkomende boodskappe	[inkomendə boədskappə]
outgoing messages	uitgaande boodskappe	[œitχāndə boədskappə]

sender	sender	[sendər]
to send (vt)	verstuur	[ferstɪr]
sending (of mail)	versending	[fersendiŋ]

| receiver | ontvanger | [ontfaŋər] |
| to receive (vt) | ontvang | [ontfaŋ] |

| correspondence | korrespondensie | [korrespondɛŋsi] |
| to correspond (vi) | korrespondeer | [korrespondeər] |

file	lêer	[lɛər]
to download (vt)	aflaai	[aflāi]
to create (vt)	skep	[skep]
to delete (vt)	uitvee	[œitfeə]
deleted (adj)	uitgevee	[œitχefeə]

connection (ADSL, etc.)	konneksie	[konneksi]
speed	spoed	[sput]
modem	modem	[modem]
access	toegang	[tuχaŋ]
port (e.g. input ~)	portaal	[portāl]

| connection (make a ~) | aansluiting | [āŋslœitiŋ] |
| to connect to … (vi) | aansluit by … | [āŋslœit baj …] |

| to select (vt) | **kies** | [kis] |
| to search (for ...) | **soek** | [suk] |

Transport

aeroplane	**vliegtuig**	[fliχtœiχ]
air ticket	**lugkaartjie**	[luχ·kārki]
airline	**lugredery**	[luχrederaj]
airport	**lughawe**	[luχhavə]
supersonic (adj)	**supersonies**	[supersonis]
captain	**kaptein**	[kaptæjn]
crew	**bemanning**	[bemanniŋ]
pilot	**piloot**	[piloət]
stewardess	**lugwaardin**	[luχ·wārdin]
navigator	**navigator**	[nafiχator]
wings	**vlerke**	[flerkə]
tail	**stert**	[stert]
cockpit	**stuurkajuit**	[stɪr·kajœit]
engine	**enjin**	[ɛndʒin]
undercarriage (landing gear)	**landingstel**	[landiŋ·stəl]
turbine	**turbine**	[turbinə]
propeller	**skroef**	[skruf]
black box	**swart boks**	[swart boks]
yoke (control column)	**stuurstang**	[stɪr·staŋ]
fuel	**brandstof**	[brantstof]
safety card	**veiligheidskaart**	[fæjliχæjts·kārt]
oxygen mask	**suurstofmasker**	[sɪrstof·maskər]
uniform	**uniform**	[uniform]
lifejacket	**reddingsbaadjie**	[rɛddiŋs·bādʒi]
parachute	**valskerm**	[fɑl·skerm]
takeoff	**opstyging**	[opstajχiŋ]
to take off (vi)	**opstyg**	[opstajχ]
runway	**landingsbaan**	[landiŋs·bān]
visibility	**uitsig**	[œitsəχ]
flight (act of flying)	**vlug**	[fluχ]
altitude	**hoogte**	[hoəχtə]
air pocket	**lugsak**	[luχsak]
seat	**sitplek**	[sitplek]
headphones	**koptelefoon**	[kop·telefoən]
folding tray (tray table)	**voutafeltjie**	[fæu·tafɛlki]
airplane window	**vliegtuigvenster**	[fliχtœiχ·fɛŋstər]
aisle	**paadjie**	[pādʒi]

142. Train

train	**trein**	[træjn]
commuter train	**voorstedelike trein**	[foərstedelikə træjn]
express train	**sneltrein**	[snɛl·træjn]
diesel locomotive	**diesellokomotief**	[disəl·lokomotif]
steam locomotive	**stoomlokomotief**	[stoəm·lokomotif]
coach, carriage	**passasierswa**	[passasirs·wa]
buffet car	**eetwa**	[eət·wa]
rails	**spoorstawe**	[spoər·stavə]
railway	**spoorweg**	[spoər·weχ]
sleeper (track support)	**dwarslêer**	[dwarslɛər]
platform (railway ~)	**perron**	[perron]
platform (~ 1, 2, etc.)	**spoor**	[spoər]
semaphore	**semafoor**	[semafoər]
station	**stasie**	[stasi]
train driver	**treindrywer**	[træjn·drajvər]
porter (of luggage)	**portier**	[portir]
carriage attendant	**kondukteur**	[konduktøər]
passenger	**passasier**	[passasir]
ticket inspector	**kondukteur**	[konduktøər]
corridor (in train)	**gang**	[χaŋ]
emergency brake	**noodrem**	[noədrem]
compartment	**kompartiment**	[kompartiment]
berth	**bed**	[bet]
upper berth	**boonste bed**	[boəŋstə bet]
lower berth	**onderste bed**	[ondərstə bet]
bed linen, bedding	**beddegoed**	[beddə·χut]
ticket	**kaartjie**	[kārki]
timetable	**diensrooster**	[diŋs·roəstər]
information display	**informasiebord**	[informasi·bort]
to leave, to depart	**vertrek**	[fertrek]
departure (of a train)	**vertrek**	[fertrek]
to arrive (ab. train)	**aankom**	[ānkom]
arrival	**aankoms**	[ānkoms]
to arrive by train	**aankom per trein**	[ānkom pər træjn]
to get on the train	**in die trein klim**	[in di træjn klim]
to get off the train	**uit die trein klim**	[œit di træjn klim]
train crash	**treinbotsing**	[træjn·botsiŋ]
to derail (vi)	**ontspoor**	[ontspoər]
steam locomotive	**stoomlokomotief**	[stoəm·lokomotif]
stoker, fireman	**stoker**	[stokər]
firebox	**stookplek**	[stoəkplek]
coal	**steenkool**	[steən·koəl]

143. Ship

ship	**skip**	[skip]
vessel	**vaartuig**	[fãrtœiχ]
steamship	**stoomboot**	[stoəm·boət]
riverboat	**rivierboot**	[rifir·boət]
cruise ship	**toerskip**	[tur·skip]
cruiser	**kruiser**	[krœisər]
yacht	**jag**	[jaχ]
tugboat	**sleepboot**	[sleəp·boət]
barge	**vragskuit**	[fraχ·skœit]
ferry	**veerboot**	[feər·boət]
sailing ship	**seilskip**	[sæjl·skip]
brigantine	**skoenerbrik**	[skunər·brik]
ice breaker	**ysbreker**	[ajs·brekər]
submarine	**duikboot**	[dœik·boət]
boat (flat-bottomed ~)	**roeiboot**	[ruiboət]
dinghy (lifeboat)	**bootjie**	[boəki]
lifeboat	**reddingsboot**	[rɛddiŋs·boət]
motorboat	**motorboot**	[motor·boət]
captain	**kaptein**	[kaptæjn]
seaman	**seeman**	[seəman]
sailor	**matroos**	[matroəs]
crew	**bemanning**	[bemanniŋ]
boatswain	**bootsman**	[boətsman]
ship's boy	**skeepsjonge**	[skeəps·joŋə]
cook	**kok**	[kok]
ship's doctor	**skeepsdokter**	[skeəps·doktər]
deck	**dek**	[dek]
mast	**mas**	[mas]
sail	**seil**	[sæjl]
hold	**skeepsruim**	[skeəps·rœim]
bow (prow)	**boeg**	[buχ]
stern	**agterstewe**	[aχtərstevə]
oar	**roeispaan**	[ruis·pãn]
screw propeller	**skroef**	[skruf]
cabin	**kajuit**	[kajœit]
wardroom	**offisierskajuit**	[offisirs·kajœit]
engine room	**enjinkamer**	[ɛndʒin·kamər]
bridge	**brug**	[bruχ]
radio room	**radiokamer**	[radio·kamər]
wave (radio)	**golf**	[χolf]
logbook	**logboek**	[loχbuk]
spyglass	**verkyker**	[ferkajkər]
bell	**bel**	[bəl]

flag	vlag	[flaχ]
hawser (mooring ~)	kabel	[kabəl]
knot (bowline, etc.)	knoop	[knoəp]

| deckrails | dekleuning | [dek·løəniŋ] |
| gangway | gangplank | [χaŋ·plank] |

anchor	anker	[ankər]
to weigh anchor	anker lig	[ankər ləχ]
to drop anchor	anker uitgooi	[ankər œitχoj]
anchor chain	ankerketting	[ankər·kɛttiŋ]

port (harbour)	hawe	[havə]
quay, wharf	kaai	[kāi]
to berth (moor)	vasmeer	[fasmeər]
to cast off	vertrek	[fertrek]

trip, voyage	reis	[ræjs]
cruise (sea trip)	cruise	[kru:s]
course (route)	koers	[kurs]
route (itinerary)	roete	[rutə]

fairway (safe water channel)	vaarwater	[fār·vatər]
shallows	sandbank	[sand·bank]
to run aground	strand	[strant]

storm	storm	[storm]
signal	sienjaal	[sinjāl]
to sink (vi)	sink	[sink]
Man overboard!	Man oorboord!	[man oərboərd!]
SOS (distress signal)	SOS	[sos]
ring buoy	reddingsboei	[rɛddiŋs·bui]

144. Airport

airport	lughawe	[luχhavə]
aeroplane	vliegtuig	[fliχtœiχ]
airline	lugredery	[luχrederaj]
air traffic controller	lugverkeersleier	[luχ·ferkeərs·læjer]

departure	vertrek	[fertrek]
arrival	aankoms	[ānkoms]
to arrive (by plane)	aankom	[ānkom]

| departure time | vertrektyd | [fertrək·tajt] |
| arrival time | aankomstyd | [ānkoms·tajt] |

| to be delayed | vertraag wees | [fertrāχ veəs] |
| flight delay | vlugvertraging | [fluχ·fertraχiŋ] |

information board	informasiebord	[informasi·bort]
information	informasie	[informasi]
to announce (vt)	aankondig	[ānkondəχ]
flight (e.g. next ~)	vlug	[fluχ]

| customs | doeane | [duanə] |
| customs officer | doeanebeampte | [duanə·beamptə] |

customs declaration	doeaneverklaring	[duanə·ferklariŋ]
to fill in (vt)	invul	[inful]
passport control	paspoortkontrole	[paspoərt·kontrolə]

luggage	bagasie	[baχasi]
hand luggage	handbagasie	[hand·baχasi]
luggage trolley	bagasiekarretjie	[baχasi·karrəki]

landing	landing	[landiŋ]
landing strip	landingsbaan	[landiŋs·bān]
to land (vi)	land	[lant]
airstair (passenger stair)	vliegtuigtrap	[fliχtœiχ·trap]

check-in	na die vertrektoonbank	[na di fertrək·toənbank]
check-in counter	vertrektoonbank	[fertrək·toənbank]
to check-in (vi)	na die vertrektoonbank gaan	[na di fertrək·toənbank χān]
boarding card	instapkaart	[instap·kārt]
departure gate	vertrekuitgang	[fertrek·œitχaŋ]

transit	transito	[traŋsito]
to wait (vt)	wag	[vaχ]
departure lounge	vertreksaal	[fertrək·sāl]
to see off	afsien	[afsin]
to say goodbye	afskeid neem	[afskæjt neəm]

145. Bicycle. Motorcycle

bicycle	fiets	[fits]
scooter	bromponie	[bromponi]
motorbike	motorfiets	[motorfits]

to go by bicycle	per fiets ry	[pər fits raj]
handlebars	stuurstang	[stʏr·staŋ]
pedal	pedaal	[pedāl]
brakes	remme	[remmə]
bicycle seat (saddle)	fietssaal	[fits·sāl]

pump	pomp	[pomp]
pannier rack	bagasierak	[baχasi·rak]
front lamp	fietslamp	[fits·lamp]
helmet	helmet	[hɛlmet]

wheel	wiel	[vil]
mudguard	modderskerm	[moddər·skerm]
rim	velling	[fɛlliŋ]
spoke	speek	[speək]

Cars

car	**motor**	[motor]
sports car	**sportmotor**	[sport·motor]
limousine	**limousine**	[limæʊsinə]
off-road vehicle	**veldvoertuig**	[fɛlt·furtœiχ]
drophead coupé (convertible)	**met afslaandak**	[met afslāndak]
minibus	**bussie**	[bussi]
ambulance	**ambulans**	[ambulaŋs]
snowplough	**sneeuploeg**	[sniʊ·pluχ]
lorry	**vragmotor**	[fraχ·motor]
road tanker	**tenkwa**	[tɛnk·wa]
van (small truck)	**bestelwa**	[bestəl·wa]
tractor unit	**padtrekker**	[pad·trɛkkər]
trailer	**aanhangwa**	[ānhaŋ·wa]
comfortable (adj)	**gemaklik**	[χemaklik]
used (adj)	**gebruik**	[χebrœik]

bonnet	**enjinkap**	[ɛndʒin·kap]
wing	**modderskerm**	[moddər·skerm]
roof	**dak**	[dak]
windscreen	**voorruit**	[foər·rœit]
rear-view mirror	**truspieël**	[tru·spiɛl]
windscreen washer	**voorruitsproer**	[foər·rœitsprur]
windscreen wipers	**ruitveërs**	[rœit·feɛrs]
side window	**syvenster**	[saj·fɛŋstər]
electric window	**vensterhyser**	[fɛŋstər·hajsər]
aerial	**lugdraad**	[luχdrāt]
sunroof	**sondak**	[sondak]
bumper	**buffer**	[buffər]
boot	**bagasiebak**	[baχasi·bak]
roof luggage rack	**dakreling**	[dak·reliŋ]
door	**deur**	[døər]
door handle	**handvatsel**	[hand·fatsəl]
door lock	**deurslot**	[døər·slot]
number plate	**nommerplaat**	[nommər·plāt]
silencer	**knaldemper**	[knal·dempər]

| petrol tank | petroltenk | [petrol·tɛnk] |
| exhaust pipe | uitlaatpyp | [œitlãt·pajp] |

accelerator	gaspedaal	[ɣas·pedãl]
pedal	pedaal	[pedãl]
accelerator pedal	gaspedaal	[ɣas·pedãl]

brake	rem	[rem]
brake pedal	rempedaal	[rem·pedãl]
to brake (use the brake)	remtrap	[remtrap]
handbrake	parkeerrem	[parkeər·rem]

clutch	koppelaar	[koppelãr]
clutch pedal	koppelaarpedaal	[koppelãr·pedãl]
clutch disc	koppelaarskyf	[koppelãr·skajf]
shock absorber	skokbreker	[skok·brekər]

wheel	wiel	[vil]
spare tyre	spaarwiel	[spãr·wil]
tyre	band	[bant]
wheel cover (hubcap)	wieldop	[wil·dop]

driving wheels	dryfwiele	[drajf·wilə]
front-wheel drive (as adj)	voorwielaandrywing	[foərwil·ãndrajviŋ]
rear-wheel drive (as adj)	agterwielaandrywing	[aχtərwil·ãndrajviŋ]
all-wheel drive (as adj)	vierwielaandrywing	[firwil·ãndrajviŋ]

gearbox	ratkas	[ratkas]
automatic (adj)	outomaties	[æʊtomatis]
mechanical (adj)	meganies	[meχanis]
gear lever	ratwisselaar	[ratwisselãr]

| headlamp | koplig | [koplǝχ] |
| headlights | kopligte | [kopliχtə] |

dipped headlights	dempstraal	[demp·strãl]
full headlights	hoofstraal	[hoəf·strãl]
brake light	remlig	[remləχ]

sidelights	parkeerlig	[parkeər·ləχ]
hazard lights	gevaarligte	[χefãr·liχtə]
fog lights	mislampe	[mis·lampə]
turn indicator	draaiwyser	[drãj·vajsər]
reversing light	trulig	[truləχ]

148. Cars. Passenger compartment

car interior	interieur	[interiøər]
leather (as adj)	leer-	[leər-]
velour (as adj)	fluweel-	[fluveəl-]
upholstery	bekleding	[beklediŋ]

| instrument (gage) | instrument | [instrument] |
| dashboard | voorpaneel | [foər·paneəl] |

| speedometer | spoedmeter | [spud·metər] |
| needle (pointer) | wyster | [vajstər] |

mileometer	afstandmeter	[afstant·metər]
indicator (sensor)	sensor	[sɛŋsor]
level	vlak	[flak]
warning light	waarskulig	[vārskuləχ]

steering wheel	stuurwiel	[stɪr·wil]
horn	toeter	[tutər]
button	knop	[knop]
switch	skakelaar	[skakəlār]

seat	sitplek	[sitplek]
backrest	rugsteun	[ruχ·støøn]
headrest	kopstut	[kopstut]
seat belt	veiligheidsgordel	[fæjliχæjts·χordəl]
to fasten the belt	die gordel vasmaak	[di χordəl fasmāk]
adjustment (of seats)	verstelling	[ferstɛlliŋ]

| airbag | lugsak | [luχsak] |
| air-conditioner | lugversorger | [luχfersorχər] |

radio	radio	[radio]
CD player	CD-speler	[se·de spelər]
to turn on	aanskakel	[āŋskakəl]
aerial	lugdraad	[luχdrāt]
glove box	paneelkassie	[paneəl·kassi]
ashtray	asbak	[asbak]

149. Cars. Engine

engine	enjin	[ɛndʒin]
motor	motor	[motor]
diesel (as adj)	diesel	[disəl]
petrol (as adj)	petrol	[petrol]

engine volume	enjininhoud	[ɛndʒin·inhæut]
power	krag	[kraχ]
horsepower	perdekrag	[perdə·kraχ]
piston	suier	[sœier]
cylinder	silinder	[silindər]
valve	klep	[klep]

injector	inspuiting	[inspœitiŋ]
generator (alternator)	generator	[χenerator]
carburettor	vergasser	[ferχassər]
motor oil	motorolie	[motor·oli]

radiator	verkoeler	[ferkulər]
coolant	koelmiddel	[kul·middəl]
cooling fan	waaier	[vājer]
battery (accumulator)	battery	[battəraj]
starter	aansitter	[āŋsittər]

| ignition | ontsteking | [ontstekiŋ] |
| sparking plug | vonkprop | [fonk·prop] |

terminal (battery ~)	pool	[poəl]
positive terminal	positiewe pool	[positivə poəl]
negative terminal	negatiewe pool	[neχativə poəl]
fuse	sekering	[sekəriŋ]

air filter	lugfilter	[luχ·filtər]
oil filter	oliefilter	[oli·filtər]
fuel filter	brandstoffilter	[brantstof·filtər]

150. Cars. Crash. Repair

car crash	motorbotsing	[motor·botsiŋ]
traffic accident	verkeersongeluk	[ferkeərs·onχəluk]
to crash (into the wall, etc.)	bots	[bots]
to get smashed up	verongeluk	[feronχəluk]
damage	skade	[skadə]
intact (unscathed)	onbeskadig	[onbeskadəχ]

breakdown	onklãr raak	[onklãr rãk]
to break down (vi)	onklãr raak	[onklãr rãk]
towrope	sleeptou	[sleəp·tæʊ]

puncture	papwiel	[pap·wil]
to have a puncture	pap wees	[pap veəs]
to pump up	oppomp	[oppomp]
pressure	druk	[druk]
to check (to examine)	nagaan	[naχãn]

repair	herstel	[herstəl]
garage (auto service shop)	garage	[χaraʒə]
spare part	onderdeel	[ondərdeəl]
part	onderdeel	[ondərdeəl]

bolt (with nut)	bout	[bæʊt]
screw (fastener)	skroef	[skruf]
nut	moer	[mur]
washer	waster	[vastər]
bearing (e.g. ball ~)	koeëllaer	[kuɛllaər]

tube	pyp	[pajp]
gasket (head ~)	pakstuk	[pakstuk]
cable, wire	kabel	[kabəl]

jack	domkrag	[domkraχ]
spanner	moersleutel	[mur·sløətəl]
hammer	hamer	[hamər]
pump	pomp	[pomp]
screwdriver	skroewedraaier	[skruvə·drãjer]

| fire extinguisher | brandblusser | [brant·blussər] |
| warning triangle | gevaardriehoek | [χefãr·drihuk] |

to stall (vi)	stol	[stol]
stall (n)	stol	[stol]
to be broken	stukkend wees	[stukkent vees]

to overheat (vi)	oorverhit	[oərferhit]
to be clogged up	verstop raak	[ferstop rāk]
to freeze up (pipes, etc.)	vries	[fris]
to burst (vi, ab. tube)	bars	[bars]

pressure	druk	[druk]
level	vlak	[flak]
slack (~ belt)	slap	[slap]

dent	duik	[dœik]
knocking noise (engine)	klopgeluid	[klop·χəlœit]
crack	kraak	[krāk]
scratch	skraap	[skrāp]

151. Cars. Road

road	pad	[pat]
motorway	deurpad	[døərpat]
highway	deurpad	[døərpat]
direction (way)	rigting	[riχtiŋ]
distance	afstand	[afstant]

bridge	brug	[bruχ]
car park	parkeerterrein	[parkeər·terræjn]
square	plein	[plæjn]
road junction	padknoop	[pad·knoəp]
tunnel	tonnel	[tonnəl]

petrol station	petrolstasie	[petrol·stasi]
car park	parkeerterrein	[parkeər·terræjn]
petrol pump	petrolpomp	[petrol·pomp]
auto repair shop	garage	[χaraʒə]
to fill up	volmaak	[folmāk]
fuel	brandstof	[brantstof]
jerrycan	petrolblik	[petrol·blik]

asphalt, tarmac	teer	[teər]
road markings	padmerktekens	[pad·merktekɛns]
kerb	randsteen	[rand·steən]
crash barrier	skutreling	[skut·reliŋ]
ditch	donga	[donχa]
roadside (shoulder)	skouer	[skæʋər]
lamppost	lamppaal	[lamp·pāl]

to drive (a car)	bestuur	[bestɪr]
to turn (e.g., ~ left)	draai	[drāi]
to make a U-turn	U-draai maak	[u-drāj māk]
reverse (~ gear)	tru-	[tru-]
to honk (vi)	toeter	[tutər]
honk (sound)	toeter	[tutər]

to get stuck (in the mud, etc.)	**vassteek**	[fassteək]
to spin the wheels	**die wiele laat tol**	[di vilə lāt tol]
to cut, to turn off (vt)	**afskakel**	[afskakəl]
speed	**spoed**	[sput]
to exceed the speed limit	**die spoedgrens oortree**	[di sputχrɛŋs oərtreə]
traffic lights	**robot**	[robot]
driving licence	**bestuurslisensie**	[bestɪrs·lisɛŋsi]
level crossing	**treinoorgang**	[træjn·oərχaŋ]
crossroads	**kruispunt**	[krœis·punt]
zebra crossing	**sebraoorgang**	[sebra·oərχaŋ]
bend, curve	**draai**	[drāi]
pedestrian precinct	**voetgangerstraat**	[futχaŋər·strāt]

PEOPLE. LIFE EVENTS

152. Holidays. Event

celebration, holiday	partytjie	[partajki]
national day	nasionale dag	[naʃionalə daχ]
public holiday	openbare vakansiedag	[openbarə fakaŋsi·daχ]
to commemorate (vt)	herdenk	[herdenk]
event (happening)	gebeurtenis	[χebøørtenis]
event (organized activity)	gebeurtenis	[χebøørtenis]
banquet (party)	banket	[banket]
reception (formal party)	onthaal	[onthāl]
feast	feesmaal	[feəs·māl]
anniversary	verjaardag	[ferjār·daχ]
jubilee	jubileum	[jubiløəm]
to celebrate (vt)	vier	[fir]
New Year	Nuwejaar	[nuvejār]
Happy New Year!	Voorspoedige Nuwejaar	[foərspudiχə nuvejār]
Father Christmas	Kersvader	[kers·fadər]
Christmas	Kersfees	[kersfeəs]
Merry Christmas!	Geseënde Kersfees	[χeseɛndə kersfeɛs]
Christmas tree	Kersboom	[kers·boəm]
fireworks (fireworks show)	vuurwerk	[fɪrwerk]
wedding	bruilof	[brœilof]
groom	bruidegom	[brœidəχom]
bride	bruid	[brœit]
to invite (vt)	uitnooi	[œitnoj]
invitation card	uitnodiging	[œitnodəχiŋ]
guest	gas	[χas]
to visit (~ your parents, etc.)	besoek	[besuk]
to meet the guests	die gaste ontmoet	[di χastə ontmut]
gift, present	present	[present]
to give (sth as present)	gee	[χeə]
to receive gifts	presente ontvang	[presentə ontfaŋ]
bouquet (of flowers)	boeket	[buket]
congratulations	gelukwense	[χelukwɛŋsə]
to congratulate (vt)	gelukwens	[χelukwɛŋs]
greetings card	geleentheidskaartjie	[χeleenthæjts·kārki]
toast	heildronk	[hæjldronk]
to offer (a drink, etc.)	aanbied	[ānbit]

champagne	sjampanje	[ʃampanje]
to enjoy oneself	jouself geniet	[jæusɛlf χenit]
merriment (gaiety)	pret	[pret]
joy (emotion)	vreugde	[frøəχdə]

| dance | dans | [daŋs] |
| to dance (vi, vt) | dans | [daŋs] |

| waltz | wals | [vals] |
| tango | tango | [tanχo] |

153. Funerals. Burial

cemetery	begraafplaas	[beχrãf·plãs]
grave, tomb	graf	[χraf]
cross	kruis	[krœis]
gravestone	grafsteen	[χrafsteən]
fence	heining	[hæjniŋ]
chapel	kapel	[kapəl]

death	dood	[doət]
to die (vi)	doodgaan	[doədχãn]
the deceased	oorledene	[oərledenə]
mourning	rou	[ræu]

to bury (vt)	begrawe	[beχravə]
undertakers	begrafnisonderneming	[beχrafnis·ondərnemiŋ]
funeral	begrafnis	[beχrafnis]

wreath	krans	[kraŋs]
coffin	doodskis	[doədskis]
hearse	lykswa	[lajks·wa]
shroud	lykkleed	[lajk·kleət]

funeral procession	begrafnisstoet	[beχrafnis·stut]
funerary urn	urn	[urn]
crematorium	krematorium	[krematorium]

obituary	doodsberig	[doəds·berəχ]
to cry (weep)	huil	[hœil]
to sob (vi)	snik	[snik]

154. War. Soldiers

platoon	peleton	[peleton]
company	kompanie	[kompani]
regiment	regiment	[reχiment]
army	leër	[leɛr]
division	divisie	[difisi]

| section, squad | afdeling | [afdeliŋ] |
| host (army) | leërskare | [leɛrskarə] |

| soldier | soldaat | [soldāt] |
| officer | offisier | [offisir] |

private	soldaat	[soldāt]
sergeant	sersant	[sersant]
lieutenant	luitenant	[lœitənant]
captain	kaptein	[kaptæjn]
major	majoor	[majoər]
colonel	kolonel	[kolonəl]
general	generaal	[χenerāl]

sailor	matroos	[matroəs]
captain	kaptein	[kaptæjn]
boatswain	bootsman	[boətsman]

artilleryman	artilleris	[artilleris]
paratrooper	valskermsoldaat	[falskerm·soldāt]
pilot	piloot	[piloət]
navigator	navigator	[nafiχator]
mechanic	werktuigkundige	[verktœiχ·kundiχə]

pioneer (sapper)	sappeur	[sappøər]
parachutist	valskermspringer	[falskerm·spriŋər]
reconnaissance scout	verkenner	[ferkɛnnər]
sniper	skerpskut	[skerp·skut]

patrol (group)	patrollie	[patrolli]
to patrol (vt)	patrolleer	[patrolleər]
sentry, guard	wag	[vaχ]

warrior	vegter	[feχtər]
patriot	patriot	[patriot]
hero	held	[hɛlt]
heroine	heldin	[hɛldin]

| traitor | verraaier | [ferrājer] |
| to betray (vt) | verraai | [ferrāi] |

| deserter | droster | [drostər] |
| to desert (vi) | dros | [dros] |

mercenary	huursoldaat	[hɪr·soldāt]
recruit	rekruteer	[rekruteər]
volunteer	vrywilliger	[frajvilliχər]

dead (n)	dooie	[doje]
wounded (n)	gewonde	[χevondə]
prisoner of war	krygsgevangene	[krajχs·χefaŋənə]

155. War. Military actions. Part 1

war	oorlog	[oərloχ]
to be at war	oorlog voer	[oərloχ fur]
civil war	burgeroorlog	[burgər·oərloχ]

treacherously (adv)	valslik	[falslik]
declaration of war	oorlogsverklaring	[oərloχs·ferklariŋ]
to declare (~ war)	oorlog verklaar	[oərloχ ferklār]
aggression	aggressie	[aχrɛssi]
to attack (invade)	aanval	[ānfal]

to invade (vt)	binneval	[binnəfal]
invader	binnevaller	[binnəfallər]
conqueror	veroweraar	[feroverār]

defence	verdediging	[ferdedəχiŋ]
to defend (a country, etc.)	verdedig	[ferdedəχ]
to defend (against …)	jouself verdedig	[jæusɛlf ferdedəχ]

enemy	vyand	[fajant]
foe, adversary	teëstander	[teɛstandər]
enemy (as adj)	vyandig	[fajandəχ]

| strategy | strategie | [strateχi] |
| tactics | taktiek | [taktik] |

order	bevel	[befəl]
command (order)	bevel	[befəl]
to order (vt)	beveel	[befeəl]
mission	opdrag	[opdraχ]
secret (adj)	geheim	[χəhæjm]

| battle | veldslag | [fɛltslaχ] |
| combat | geveg | [χefeχ] |

attack	aanval	[ānfal]
charge (assault)	bestorming	[bestormiŋ]
to storm (vt)	bestorm	[bestorm]
siege (to be under ~)	beleg	[beleχ]

| offensive (n) | aanval | [ānfal] |
| to go on the offensive | tot die offensief oorgaan | [tot di offɛŋsif oərχān] |

| retreat | terugtrekking | [teruχ·trɛkkiŋ] |
| to retreat (vi) | terugtrek | [teruχtrek] |

| encirclement | omsingeling | [omsinχəliŋ] |
| to encircle (vt) | omsingel | [omsiŋəl] |

bombing (by aircraft)	bombardement	[bombardement]
to bomb (vt)	bombardeer	[bombardeər]
explosion	ontploffing	[ontploffiŋ]

| shot | skoot | [skoət] |
| firing (burst of ~) | skiet | [skit] |

to aim (to point a weapon)	mik op	[mik op]
to point (a gun)	rig	[riχ]
to hit (the target)	tref	[tref]
to sink (~ a ship)	sink	[sink]
hole (in a ship)	gat	[χat]

to founder, to sink (vi)	sink	[sink]
front (war ~)	front	[front]
evacuation	evakuasie	[ɛfakuasi]
to evacuate (vt)	evakueer	[ɛfakueər]

trench	loopgraaf	[loəpχrāf]
barbed wire	doringdraad	[doriŋ·drāt]
barrier (anti tank ~)	versperring	[fersperriŋ]
watchtower	wagtoring	[vaχ·toriŋ]

military hospital	militêre hospitaal	[militærə hospitāl]
to wound (vt)	wond	[vont]
wound	wond	[vont]
wounded (n)	gewonde	[χevondə]
to be wounded	gewond	[χevont]
serious (wound)	ernstig	[ɛrnstəχ]

156. Weapons

weapons	wapens	[vapɛns]
firearms	vuurwapens	[fɪr·vapɛns]
cold weapons (knives, etc.)	messe	[mɛssə]

chemical weapons	chemiese wapens	[χemisə vapɛns]
nuclear (adj)	kern-	[kern-]
nuclear weapons	kernwapens	[kern·vapɛns]

| bomb | bom | [bom] |
| atomic bomb | atoombom | [atoəm·bom] |

pistol (gun)	pistool	[pistoəl]
rifle	geweer	[χeveər]
submachine gun	aanvalsgeweer	[ānvals·χeveər]
machine gun	masjiengeweer	[maʃin·χeveər]

muzzle	loop	[loəp]
barrel	loop	[loəp]
calibre	kaliber	[kalibər]

trigger	sneller	[snɛllər]
sight (aiming device)	visier	[fisir]
magazine	magasyn	[maχasajn]
butt (shoulder stock)	kolf	[kolf]

| hand grenade | handgranaat | [hand·χranāt] |
| explosive | springstof | [spriŋstof] |

bullet	koeël	[kuɛl]
cartridge	patroon	[patroən]
charge	lading	[ladiŋ]
ammunition	ammunisie	[ammunisi]

| bomber (aircraft) | bomwerper | [bom·werpər] |
| fighter | straalvegter | [strāl·feχtər] |

helicopter	helikopter	[helikoptər]
anti-aircraft gun	lugafweer	[luχafweər]
tank	tenk	[tɛnk]
tank gun	tenkkanon	[tɛnk·kanon]

artillery	artillerie	[artilleri]
gun (cannon, howitzer)	kanon	[kanon]
to lay (a gun)	aanlê	[ānlɛ:]

shell (projectile)	projektiel	[projektil]
mortar bomb	mortierbom	[mortir·bom]
mortar	mortier	[mortir]
splinter (shell fragment)	skrapnel	[skrapnəl]

submarine	duikboot	[dœik·boət]
torpedo	torpedo	[torpedo]
missile	vuurpyl	[fɪr·pajl]

to load (gun)	laai	[lāi]
to shoot (vi)	skiet	[skit]
to point at (the cannon)	rig op	[riχ op]
bayonet	bajonet	[bajonet]

rapier	rapier	[rapir]
sabre (e.g. cavalry ~)	sabel	[sabəl]
spear (weapon)	spies	[spis]
bow	boog	[boəχ]
arrow	pyl	[pajl]
musket	musket	[musket]
crossbow	kruisboog	[krœis·boəχ]

157. Ancient people

primitive (prehistoric)	primitief	[primitif]
prehistoric (adj)	prehistories	[prehistoris]
ancient (~ civilization)	antiek	[antik]

Stone Age	Steentydperk	[steən·tajtperk]
Bronze Age	Bronstydperk	[brɔŋs·tajtperk]
Ice Age	Ystydperk	[ajs·tajtperk]

tribe	stam	[stam]
cannibal	mensvreter	[mɛŋs·fretər]
hunter	jagter	[jaχtər]
to hunt (vi, vt)	jag	[jaχ]
mammoth	mammoet	[mammut]

cave	grot	[χrot]
fire	vuur	[fɪr]
campfire	kampvuur	[kampfɪr]
cave painting	rotstekening	[rots·tekəniŋ]

| tool (e.g. stone axe) | werktuig | [verktœiχ] |
| spear | spies | [spis] |

stone axe	**klipbyl**	[klip·bajl]
to be at war	**oorlog voer**	[oərloχ fur]
to domesticate (vt)	**tem**	[tem]
idol	**afgod**	[afχot]
to worship (vt)	**aanbid**	[ānbit]
superstition	**bygeloof**	[bajχəloəf]
rite	**ritueel**	[ritueəl]
evolution	**evolusie**	[ɛfolusi]
development	**ontwikkeling**	[ontwikkeliŋ]
disappearance (extinction)	**verdwyning**	[ferdwajniŋ]
to adapt oneself	**jou aanpas**	[jæʊ ānpas]
archaeology	**argeologie**	[arχeoloχi]
archaeologist	**argeoloog**	[arχeoloəχ]
archaeological (adj)	**argeologies**	[arχeoloχis]
excavation site	**opgrawingsplek**	[opχraviŋs·plek]
excavations	**opgrawingsplekke**	[opχraviŋs·plɛkkə]
find (object)	**vonds**	[fonds]
fragment	**fragment**	[fraχment]

158. Middle Ages

people (ethnic group)	**volk**	[folk]
peoples	**bevolking**	[befolkiŋ]
tribe	**stam**	[stam]
tribes	**stamme**	[stammə]
barbarians	**barbare**	[barbarə]
Gauls	**Galliërs**	[χalliɛrs]
Goths	**Gote**	[χote]
Slavs	**Slawe**	[slavə]
Vikings	**Vikings**	[vikiŋs]
Romans	**Romeine**	[romæjnə]
Roman (adj)	**Romeins**	[romæjns]
Byzantines	**Bisantyne**	[bisantajnə]
Byzantium	**Bisantium**	[bisantium]
Byzantine (adj)	**Bisantyns**	[bisantajns]
emperor	**keiser**	[kæjsər]
leader, chief (tribal ~)	**leier**	[læjer]
powerful (~ king)	**magtig**	[maχtəχ]
king	**koning**	[koniŋ]
ruler (sovereign)	**heerser**	[heərsər]
knight	**ridder**	[riddər]
feudal lord	**feodale heerser**	[feodalə heərsər]
feudal (adj)	**feodaal**	[feodāl]
vassal	**vasal**	[fasal]
duke	**hertog**	[hertoχ]

earl	graaf	[χrãf]
baron	baron	[baron]
bishop	biskop	[biskop]

armour	harnas	[harnas]
shield	skild	[skilt]
sword	swaard	[swãrt]
visor	visier	[fisir]
chainmail	maliehemp	[mali·hemp]

Crusade	Kruistog	[krœis·toχ]
crusader	kruisvaarder	[krœis·fãrdər]

territory	gebied	[χebit]
to attack (invade)	aanval	[ãnfal]
to conquer (vt)	verower	[ferovər]
to occupy (invade)	beset	[beset]

siege (to be under ~)	beleg	[beleχ]
besieged (adj)	beleërde	[beleɛrdə]
to besiege (vt)	beleër	[beleɛr]

inquisition	inkwisisie	[inkvisisi]
inquisitor	inkwisiteur	[inkvisitøər]
torture	marteling	[martəliŋ]
cruel (adj)	wreed	[vreət]
heretic	ketter	[kɛttər]
heresy	kettery	[kɛtteraj]

seafaring	seevaart	[seə·fãrt]
pirate	piraat, seerower	[pirãt], [seə·rovər]
piracy	piratery, seerowery	[pirateraj], [seə·roveraj]
boarding (attack)	enter	[ɛntər]
loot, booty	buit	[bœit]
treasure	skatte	[skattə]

discovery	ontdekking	[ontdɛkkiŋ]
to discover (new land, etc.)	ontdek	[ontdek]
expedition	ekspedisie	[ɛkspedisi]

musketeer	musketier	[musketir]
cardinal	kardinaal	[kardinãl]
heraldry	heraldiek	[heraldik]
heraldic (adj)	heraldies	[heraldis]

159. Leader. Chief. Authorities

king	koning	[koniŋ]
queen	koningin	[koniŋin]
royal (adj)	koninklik	[koninklik]
kingdom	koninkryk	[koninkrajk]

prince	prins	[prins]
princess	prinses	[prinsəs]

president	president	[president]
vice-president	vise-president	[fise-president]
senator	senator	[senator]

monarch	monarg	[monarχ]
ruler (sovereign)	heerser	[heərsər]
dictator	diktator	[diktator]
tyrant	tiran	[tiran]
magnate	magnaat	[maχnãt]

director	direkteur	[direktøər]
chief	baas	[bãs]
manager (director)	bestuurder	[bestɪrdər]
boss	baas	[bãs]
owner	eienaar	[æjenãr]

leader	leier	[læjer]
head (~ of delegation)	hoof	[hoəf]
authorities	outoriteite	[æutoritæjtə]
superiors	hoofde	[hoəfdə]

governor	goewerneur	[χuvernøər]
consul	konsul	[kɔŋsul]
diplomat	diplomaat	[diplomãt]
mayor	burgermeester	[burgər·meəstər]
sheriff	sheriff	[sheriff]

emperor	keiser	[kæjsər]
tsar, czar	tsaar	[tsãr]
pharaoh	farao	[farao]
khan	kan	[kan]

160. Breaking the law. Criminals. Part 1

bandit	bandiet	[bandit]
crime	misdaad	[misdãt]
criminal (person)	misdadiger	[misdadiχər]

thief	dief	[dif]
to steal (vi, vt)	steel	[steəl]
stealing (larceny)	steel	[steəl]
theft	diefstal	[difstal]

to kidnap (vt)	ontvoer	[ontfur]
kidnapping	ontvoering	[ontfuriŋ]
kidnapper	ontvoerder	[ontfurdər]

| ransom | losgeld | [losχɛlt] |
| to demand ransom | losgeld eis | [losχɛlt æjs] |

to rob (vt)	besteel	[besteəl]
robbery	oorval	[oərfal]
robber	boef	[buf]
to extort (vt)	afpers	[afpers]

| extortionist | afperser | [afpersər] |
| extortion | afpersing | [afpersiŋ] |

to murder, to kill	vermoor	[fermoər]
murder	moord	[moərt]
murderer	moordenaar	[moərdenãr]

gunshot	skoot	[skoət]
to shoot to death	doodskiet	[doədskit]
to shoot (vi)	skiet	[skit]
shooting	skietery	[skiteraj]

incident (fight, etc.)	insident	[insident]
fight, brawl	geveg	[χefeχ]
Help!	Help!	[hɛlp!]
victim	slagoffer	[slaχoffər]

to damage (vt)	beskadig	[beskadəχ]
damage	skade	[skadə]
dead body, corpse	lyk	[lajk]
grave (~ crime)	ernstig	[ɛrnstəχ]

to attack (vt)	aanval	[ãnfal]
to beat (to hit)	slaan	[slãn]
to beat up	platslaan	[platslãn]
to take (rob of sth)	vat	[fat]

to stab to death	doodsteek	[doədsteək]
to maim (vt)	vermink	[fermink]
to wound (vt)	wond	[vont]

blackmail	afpersing	[afpersiŋ]
to blackmail (vt)	afpers	[afpers]
blackmailer	afperser	[afpersər]

protection racket	beskermingswendelary	[beskermiŋ·swendəlaraj]
racketeer	afperser	[afpersər]
gangster	boef	[buf]
mafia	mafia	[mafia]

pickpocket	sakkeroller	[sakkerollər]
burglar	inbreker	[inbrekər]
smuggling	smokkel	[smokkəl]
smuggler	smokkelaar	[smokkəlãr]

forgery	vervalsing	[ferfalsiŋ]
to forge (counterfeit)	verval	[ferfal]
fake (forged)	vals	[fals]

161. Breaking the law. Criminals. Part 2

rape	verkragting	[ferkraχtiŋ]
to rape (vt)	verkrag	[ferkraχ]
rapist	verkragter	[ferkraχtər]

maniac	**maniak**	[maniak]
prostitute (fem.)	**prostituut**	[prostitɪt]
prostitution	**prostitusie**	[prostitusi]
pimp	**pooier**	[pojer]
drug addict	**dwelmslaaf**	[dwɛlm·slãf]
drug dealer	**dwelmhandelaar**	[dwɛlm·handəlãr]
to blow up (bomb)	**opblaas**	[opblãs]
explosion	**ontploffing**	[ontploffiŋ]
to set fire	**aan die brand steek**	[ãn di brant steek]
arsonist	**brandstigter**	[brant·stiχtər]
terrorism	**terrorisme**	[terrorismə]
terrorist	**terroris**	[terroris]
hostage	**gyselaar**	[χajsəlãr]
to swindle (deceive)	**bedrieg**	[bedrəχ]
swindle, deception	**bedrog**	[bedroχ]
swindler	**bedrieër**	[bedriɛr]
to bribe (vt)	**omkoop**	[omkoəp]
bribery	**omkopery**	[omkoperaj]
bribe	**omkoopgeld**	[omkoəp·χɛlt]
poison	**gif**	[χif]
to poison (vt)	**vergiftig**	[ferχiftəχ]
to poison oneself	**jouself vergiftig**	[jæʊsɛlf ferχiftəχ]
suicide (act)	**selfmoord**	[sɛlfmoərt]
suicide (person)	**selfmoordenaar**	[sɛlfmoərdenãr]
to threaten (vt)	**dreig**	[dræjχ]
threat	**dreigement**	[dræjχement]
attempt (attack)	**aanslag**	[ãŋslaχ]
to steal (a car)	**steel**	[steəl]
to hijack (a plane)	**kaap**	[kãp]
revenge	**wraak**	[vrãk]
to avenge (get revenge)	**wreek**	[vreək]
to torture (vt)	**martel**	[martəl]
torture	**marteling**	[martəliŋ]
to torment (vt)	**folter**	[foltər]
pirate	**piraat, seerower**	[pirãt], [seə·rovər]
hooligan	**skollie**	[skolli]
armed (adj)	**gewapen**	[χevapen]
violence	**geweld**	[χevɛlt]
illegal (unlawful)	**onwettig**	[onwɛttəχ]
spying (espionage)	**spioenasie**	[spiunasi]
to spy (vi)	**spioeneer**	[spiuneər]

162. Police. Law. Part 1

justice	justisie	[jestisi]
court (see you in ~)	geregshof	[χereχshof]
judge	regter	[reχter]
jurors	jurielede	[jurilede]
jury trial	jurieregspraak	[juri·reχsprāk]
to judge, to try (vt)	bereg	[bereχ]
lawyer, barrister	advokaat	[adfokāt]
defendant	beklaagde	[beklāχde]
dock	beklaagdebank	[beklāχde·bank]
charge	aanklag	[ānklaχ]
accused	beskuldigde	[beskuldiχde]
sentence	vonnis	[fonnis]
to sentence (vt)	veroordeel	[feroerdeel]
guilty (culprit)	skuldig	[skuldeχ]
to punish (vt)	straf	[straf]
punishment	straf	[straf]
fine (penalty)	boete	[bute]
life imprisonment	lewenslange gevangenisstraf	[levɛŋslaŋe χefaŋenis·straf]
death penalty	doodstraf	[doedstraf]
electric chair	elektriese stoel	[ɛlektrise stul]
gallows	galg	[χalχ]
to execute (vt)	eksekuteer	[ɛksekuteer]
execution	eksekusie	[ɛksekusi]
prison	tronk	[tronk]
cell	sel	[səl]
escort (convoy)	eskort	[ɛskort]
prison officer	tronkbewaarder	[tronk·bevārder]
prisoner	gevangene	[χefaŋene]
handcuffs	handboeie	[hant·buje]
to handcuff (vt)	in die boeie slaan	[in di buje slān]
prison break	ontsnapping	[ontsnappiŋ]
to break out (vi)	ontsnap	[ontsnap]
to disappear (vi)	verdwyn	[ferdwajn]
to release (from prison)	vrylaat	[frajlāt]
amnesty	amnestie	[amnesti]
police	polisie	[polisi]
police officer	polisieman	[polisi·man]
police station	polisiestasie	[polisi·stasi]
truncheon	knuppel	[knuppel]
megaphone (loudhailer)	megafoon	[meχafoen]

patrol car	patrolliemotor	[patrolli·motor]
siren	sirene	[sirenə]
to turn on the siren	die sirene aanskakel	[di sirenə āŋskakəl]
siren call	sirenegeloei	[sirenə·χelui]

crime scene	misdaadtoneel	[misdād·toneəl]
witness	getuie	[χetœiə]
freedom	vryheid	[frajhæjt]
accomplice	medepligtige	[medə·pliχtiχə]
to flee (vi)	ontvlug	[ontfluχ]
trace (to leave a ~)	spoor	[spoər]

163. Police. Law. Part 2

search (investigation)	soektog	[suktoχ]
to look for ...	soek ...	[suk ...]
suspicion	verdenking	[ferdɛnkiŋ]
suspicious (e.g., ~ vehicle)	verdag	[ferdaχ]
to stop (cause to halt)	teëhou	[teɕhæʊ]
to detain (keep in custody)	aanhou	[ānhæʊ]

case (lawsuit)	hofsaak	[hofsāk]
investigation	ondersoek	[ondərsuk]
detective	speurder	[spøərdər]
investigator	speurder	[spøərdər]
hypothesis	hipotese	[hipotesə]

motive	motief	[motif]
interrogation	ondervraging	[ondərfraχiŋ]
to interrogate (vt)	ondervra	[ondərfra]
to question	verhoor	[ferhoər]
(~ neighbors, etc.)		
check (identity ~)	kontroleer	[kontroleər]

round-up (raid)	klopjag	[klopjaχ]
search (~ warrant)	huissoeking	[hœis·sukiŋ]
chase (pursuit)	agtervolging	[aχtərfolχiŋ]
to pursue, to chase	agtervolg	[aχtərfolχ]
to track (a criminal)	opspoor	[opspoər]

arrest	inhegtenisneming	[inheχtenis·nemiŋ]
to arrest (sb)	arresteer	[arresteər]
to catch (thief, etc.)	vang	[faŋ]
capture	opsporing	[opsporiŋ]

document	dokument	[dokument]
proof (evidence)	bewys	[bevajs]
to prove (vt)	bewys	[bevajs]
footprint	voetspoor	[futspoər]
fingerprints	vingerafdrukke	[fiŋər·afdrukkə]
piece of evidence	bewysstuk	[bevajs·stuk]

| alibi | alibi | [alibi] |
| innocent (not guilty) | onskuldig | [oŋskuldəχ] |

| injustice | onreg | [onreχ] |
| unjust, unfair (adj) | onregverdig | [onreχferdəχ] |

criminal (adj)	krimineel	[krimineel]
to confiscate (vt)	in beslag neem	[in beslaχ neem]
drug (illegal substance)	dwelm	[dwɛlm]
weapon, gun	wapen	[vapen]
to disarm (vt)	ontwapen	[ontvapen]
to order (command)	beveel	[befeel]
to disappear (vi)	verdwyn	[ferdwajn]

law	wet	[vet]
legal, lawful (adj)	wettig	[vɛttəχ]
illegal, illicit (adj)	onwettig	[onwɛttəχ]

| responsibility (blame) | verantwoordelikheid | [ferant·voərdelikhæjt] |
| responsible (adj) | verantwoordelik | [ferant·voərdelik] |

NATURE

The Earth. Part 1

164. Outer space

space	kosmos	[kosmos]
space (as adj)	kosmies	[kosmis]
outer space	buitenste ruimte	[bœitɛŋstə rajmtə]
world	wêreld	[værɛlt]
universe	heelal	[heəlal]
galaxy	sterrestelsel	[sterrə·stɛlsəl]
star	ster	[ster]
constellation	sterrebeeld	[sterrə·beəlt]
planet	planeet	[planeət]
satellite	satelliet	[satɛllit]
meteorite	meteoriet	[meteorit]
comet	komeet	[komeət]
asteroid	asteroïed	[asteroïət]
orbit	baan	[bān]
to revolve	draai	[drāi]
(~ around the Earth)		
atmosphere	atmosfeer	[atmosfeər]
the Sun	die Son	[di son]
solar system	sonnestelsel	[sonnə·stɛlsəl]
solar eclipse	sonsverduistering	[sɔŋs·ferdœisteriŋ]
the Earth	die Aarde	[di ārdə]
the Moon	die Maan	[di mān]
Mars	Mars	[mars]
Venus	Venus	[fenus]
Jupiter	Jupiter	[jupitər]
Saturn	Saturnus	[saturnus]
Mercury	Mercurius	[merkurius]
Uranus	Uranus	[uranus]
Neptune	Neptunus	[neptunus]
Pluto	Pluto	[pluto]
Milky Way	Melkweg	[melk·wex]
Great Bear (Ursa Major)	Groot Beer	[xroət beər]
North Star	Poolster	[poəl·stər]
Martian	marsbewoner	[mars·bevonər]

extraterrestrial (n)	**buiteaardse wese**	[bœitə·ārdsə vesə]
alien	**ruimtewese**	[rœimtə·vesə]
flying saucer	**vlieënde skottel**	[fliɛndə skottəl]
spaceship	**ruimteskip**	[rœimtə·skip]
space station	**ruimtestasie**	[rœimtə·stasi]
blast-off	**vertrek**	[fertrek]
engine	**enjin**	[ɛndʒin]
nozzle	**uitlaatpyp**	[œitlāt·pajp]
fuel	**brandstof**	[brantstof]
cockpit, flight deck	**stuurkajuit**	[stɪr·kajœit]
aerial	**lugdraad**	[luχdrāt]
porthole	**patryspoort**	[patrajs·poərt]
solar panel	**sonpaneel**	[son·paneəl]
spacesuit	**ruimtepak**	[rœimtə·pak]
weightlessness	**gewigloosheid**	[χeviχloəshæjt]
oxygen	**suurstof**	[sɪrstof]
docking (in space)	**koppeling**	[koppeliŋ]
to dock (vi, vt)	**koppel**	[koppəl]
observatory	**observatorium**	[observatorium]
telescope	**teleskoop**	[teleskoəp]
to observe (vt)	**waarneem**	[vārneəm]
to explore (vt)	**eksploreer**	[ɛksploreər]

165. The Earth

the Earth	**die Aarde**	[di ārdə]
the globe (the Earth)	**die aardbol**	[di ārdbol]
planet	**planeet**	[planeət]
atmosphere	**atmosfeer**	[atmosfeər]
geography	**geografie**	[χeoχrafi]
nature	**natuur**	[natɪr]
globe (table ~)	**aardbol**	[ārd·bol]
map	**kaart**	[kārt]
atlas	**atlas**	[atlas]
Europe	**Europa**	[øəropa]
Asia	**Asië**	[asiɛ]
Africa	**Afrika**	[afrika]
Australia	**Australië**	[ɔustraliɛ]
America	**Amerika**	[amerika]
North America	**Noord-Amerika**	[noərd-amerika]
South America	**Suid-Amerika**	[sœid-amerika]
Antarctica	**Suidpool**	[sœid·poəl]
the Arctic	**Noordpool**	[noərd·poəl]

166. Cardinal directions

north	noorde	[noərdə]
to the north	na die noorde	[na di noərdə]
in the north	in die noorde	[in di noərdə]
northern (adj)	noordelik	[noərdəlik]
south	suide	[sœidə]
to the south	na die suide	[na di sœidə]
in the south	in die suide	[in di sœidə]
southern (adj)	suidelik	[sœidəlik]
west	weste	[vestə]
to the west	na die weste	[na di vestə]
in the west	in die weste	[in di vestə]
western (adj)	westelik	[vestelik]
east	ooste	[oəstə]
to the east	na die ooste	[na di oəstə]
in the east	in die ooste	[in di oəstə]
eastern (adj)	oostelik	[oəstəlik]

167. Sea. Ocean

sea	see	[seə]
ocean	oseaan	[oseãn]
gulf (bay)	golf	[χolf]
straits	straat	[strãt]
land (solid ground)	land	[lant]
continent (mainland)	kontinent	[kontinent]
island	eiland	[æjlant]
peninsula	skiereiland	[skir·æjlant]
archipelago	argipel	[arχipəl]
bay, cove	baai	[bãi]
harbour	hawe	[havə]
lagoon	strandmeer	[strand·meər]
cape	kaap	[kãp]
atoll	atol	[atol]
reef	rif	[rif]
coral	koraal	[korãl]
coral reef	koraalrif	[korãl·rif]
deep (adj)	diep	[dip]
depth (deep water)	diepte	[diptə]
abyss	afgrond	[afχront]
trench (e.g. Mariana ~)	trog	[troχ]
current (Ocean ~)	stroming	[strominŋ]
to surround (bathe)	omring	[omrinŋ]

| shore | oewer | [uvər] |
| coast | kus | [kus] |

flow (flood tide)	hoogwater	[hoəχ·vatər]
ebb (ebb tide)	laagwater	[lāχ·vatər]
shoal	sandbank	[sand·bank]
bottom (~ of the sea)	bodem	[bodem]

wave	golf	[χolf]
crest (~ of a wave)	kruin	[krœin]
spume (sea foam)	skuim	[skœim]

storm (sea storm)	storm	[storm]
hurricane	orkaan	[orkān]
tsunami	tsunami	[tsunami]
calm (dead ~)	windstilte	[vindstiltə]
quiet, calm (adj)	kalm	[kalm]

| pole | pool | [poəl] |
| polar (adj) | polêr | [polær] |

latitude	breedtegraad	[breədtə·χrāt]
longitude	lengtegraad	[leŋtə·χrāt]
parallel	parallel	[paralləl]
equator	ewenaar	[ɛvenār]

sky	hemel	[heməl]
horizon	horison	[horison]
air	lug	[luχ]

lighthouse	vuurtoring	[fɪrtoriŋ]
to dive (vi)	duik	[dœik]
to sink (ab. boat)	sink	[sink]
treasure	skatte	[skattə]

168. Mountains

mountain	berg	[berχ]
mountain range	bergreeks	[berχ·reəks]
mountain ridge	bergrug	[berχ·ruχ]

summit, top	top	[top]
peak	piek	[pik]
foot (~ of the mountain)	voet	[fut]
slope (mountainside)	helling	[hɛlliŋ]

volcano	vulkaan	[fulkān]
active volcano	aktiewe vulkaan	[aktivə fulkān]
dormant volcano	rustende vulkaan	[rustendə fulkān]

eruption	uitbarsting	[œitbarstiŋ]
crater	krater	[kratər]
magma	magma	[maχma]
lava	lawa	[lava]

molten (~ lava)	gloeiende	[χlujendə]
canyon	diepkloof	[dip·kloəf]
gorge	kloof	[kloəf]
crevice	skeur	[skøər]
abyss (chasm)	afgrond	[afχront]

pass, col	bergpas	[berχ·pas]
plateau	plato	[plato]
cliff	krans	[kraŋs]
hill	kop	[kop]

glacier	gletser	[χletsər]
waterfall	waterval	[vatər·fal]
geyser	geiser	[χæjsər]
lake	meer	[meər]

plain	vlakte	[flaktə]
landscape	landskap	[landskap]
echo	eggo	[εχχo]

alpinist	alpinis	[alpinis]
rock climber	bergklimmer	[berχ·klimmər]
to conquer (in climbing)	baasraak	[bāsrāk]
climb (an easy ~)	beklimming	[beklimmiŋ]

169. Rivers

river	rivier	[rifir]
spring (natural source)	bron	[bron]
riverbed (river channel)	rivierbed	[rifir·bet]
basin (river valley)	stroomgebied	[stroəm·χebit]
to flow into ...	uitmond in ...	[œitmont in ...]

| tributary | syrivier | [saj·rifir] |
| bank (river ~) | oewer | [uvər] |

current (stream)	stroming	[stromiŋ]
downstream (adv)	stroomafwaarts	[stroəm·afvārts]
upstream (adv)	stroomopwaarts	[stroəm·opvārts]

inundation	oorstroming	[oərstromiŋ]
flooding	oorstroming	[oərstromiŋ]
to overflow (vi)	oor sy walle loop	[oər saj vallə loəp]
to flood (vt)	oorstroom	[oərstroəm]

| shallow (shoal) | sandbank | [sand·bank] |
| rapids | stroomversnellings | [stroəm·fersnɛlliŋs] |

dam	damwal	[dam·wal]
canal	kanaal	[kanāl]
reservoir (artificial lake)	opgaardam	[opχār·dam]
sluice, lock	sluis	[slœis]
water body (pond, etc.)	dam	[dam]
swamp (marshland)	moeras	[muras]

bog, marsh	**vlei**	[flæj]
whirlpool	**draaikolk**	[drāj·kolk]
stream (brook)	**spruit**	[sprœit]
drinking (ab. water)	**drink-**	[drink-]
fresh (~ water)	**vars**	[fars]
ice	**ys**	[ajs]
to freeze over (ab. river, etc.)	**bevries**	[befris]

170. Forest

forest, wood	**bos**	[bos]
forest (as adj)	**bos-**	[bos-]
thick forest	**woud**	[væʊt]
grove	**boord**	[boərt]
forest clearing	**oopte**	[oəptə]
thicket	**struikgewas**	[strœik·ɣevas]
scrubland	**struikveld**	[strœik·fɛlt]
footpath (troddenpath)	**paadjie**	[pādʒi]
gully	**donga**	[donɣa]
tree	**boom**	[boəm]
leaf	**blaar**	[blār]
leaves (foliage)	**blare**	[blarə]
fall of leaves	**val van die blare**	[fal fan di blarə]
to fall (ab. leaves)	**val**	[fal]
top (of the tree)	**boomtop**	[boəm·top]
branch	**tak**	[tak]
bough	**tak**	[tak]
bud (on shrub, tree)	**knop**	[knop]
needle (of the pine tree)	**naald**	[nālt]
fir cone	**dennebol**	[dɛnnə·bol]
tree hollow	**holte**	[holtə]
nest	**nes**	[nes]
burrow (animal hole)	**gat**	[ɣat]
trunk	**stam**	[stam]
root	**wortel**	[vortəl]
bark	**bas**	[bas]
moss	**mos**	[mos]
to uproot (remove trees or tree stumps)	**ontwortel**	[ontwortəl]
to chop down	**omkap**	[omkap]
to deforest (vt)	**ontbos**	[ontbos]
tree stump	**boomstomp**	[boəm·stomp]
campfire	**kampvuur**	[kampfɪr]

forest fire	**bosbrand**	[bos·brant]
to extinguish (vt)	**blus**	[blus]

forest ranger	**boswagter**	[bos·waχtər]
protection	**beskerming**	[beskermiŋ]
to protect (~ nature)	**beskerm**	[beskerm]
poacher	**wildstroper**	[vilt·stropər]
steel trap	**slagyster**	[slaχ·ajstər]

to gather, to pick (vt)	**pluk**	[pluk]
to lose one's way	**verdwaal**	[ferdwāl]

171. Natural resources

natural resources	**natuurlike bronne**	[natɪrlikə bronnə]
minerals	**minerale**	[mineralə]
deposits	**lae**	[laə]
field (e.g. oilfield)	**veld**	[fɛlt]

to mine (extract)	**myn**	[majn]
mining (extraction)	**myn**	[majn]
ore	**erts**	[ɛrts]
mine (e.g. for coal)	**myn**	[majn]
shaft (mine ~)	**mynskag**	[majn·skaχ]
miner	**mynwerker**	[majn·werkər]

gas (natural ~)	**gas**	[χas]
gas pipeline	**gaspyp**	[χas·pajp]

oil (petroleum)	**olie**	[oli]
oil pipeline	**olipypleiding**	[oli·pajp·læjdiŋ]
oil well	**oliebron**	[oli·bron]
derrick (tower)	**boortoring**	[boər·toriŋ]
tanker	**tenkskip**	[tɛnk·skip]

sand	**sand**	[sant]
limestone	**kalksteen**	[kalksteən]
gravel	**gruis**	[χrœis]
peat	**veengrond**	[feənχront]
clay	**klei**	[klæj]
coal	**steenkool**	[steən·koəl]

iron (ore)	**yster**	[ajstər]
gold	**goud**	[χæʊt]
silver	**silwer**	[silwər]
nickel	**nikkel**	[nikkəl]
copper	**koper**	[kopər]

zinc	**sink**	[sink]
manganese	**mangaan**	[manχān]
mercury	**kwik**	[kwik]
lead	**lood**	[loət]
mineral	**mineraal**	[minerāl]
crystal	**kristal**	[kristal]

| marble | **marmer** | [marmər] |
| uranium | **uraan** | [urãn] |

The Earth. Part 2

172. Weather

weather	**weer**	[veər]
weather forecast	**weersvoorspelling**	[veərs·foərspɛliŋ]
temperature	**temperatuur**	[temperatɪr]
thermometer	**termometer**	[termometər]
barometer	**barometer**	[barometər]
humid (adj)	**klam**	[klam]
humidity	**vogtigheid**	[foχtiχæjt]
heat (extreme ~)	**hitte**	[hittə]
hot (torrid)	**heet**	[heət]
it's hot	**dis vrekwarm**	[dis frekvarm]
it's warm	**dit is warm**	[dit is varm]
warm (moderately hot)	**louwarm**	[læʊvarm]
it's cold	**dis koud**	[dis kæʊt]
cold (adj)	**koud**	[kæʊt]
sun	**son**	[son]
to shine (vi)	**skyn**	[skajn]
sunny (day)	**sonnig**	[sonnəχ]
to come up (vi)	**opkom**	[opkom]
to set (vi)	**ondergaan**	[ondərχān]
cloud	**wolk**	[volk]
cloudy (adj)	**bewolk**	[bevolk]
rain cloud	**reënwolk**	[reɛn·wolk]
somber (gloomy)	**somber**	[sombər]
rain	**reën**	[reɛn]
it's raining	**dit reën**	[dit reɛn]
rainy (~ day, weather)	**reënerig**	[reɛnerəχ]
to drizzle (vi)	**motreën**	[motreɛn]
pouring rain	**stortbui**	[stortbœi]
downpour	**reënvlaag**	[reɛn·flāχ]
heavy (e.g. ~ rain)	**swaar**	[swār]
puddle	**poeletjie**	[puləki]
to get wet (in rain)	**nat word**	[nat vort]
fog (mist)	**mis**	[mis]
foggy	**mistig**	[mistəχ]
snow	**sneeu**	[sniʊ]
it's snowing	**dit sneeu**	[dit sniʊ]

173. Severe weather. Natural disasters

thunderstorm	**donderstorm**	[dondər·storm]
lightning (~ strike)	**weerlig**	[veərləχ]
to flash (vi)	**flits**	[flits]
thunder	**donder**	[dondər]
to thunder (vi)	**donder**	[dondər]
it's thundering	**dit donder**	[dit dondər]
hail	**hael**	[haəl]
it's hailing	**dit hael**	[dit haəl]
to flood (vt)	**oorstroom**	[oərstroəm]
flood, inundation	**oorstroming**	[oərstromiŋ]
earthquake	**aardbewing**	[ārd·beviŋ]
tremor, shoke	**aardskok**	[ārd·skok]
epicentre	**episentrum**	[ɛpisentrum]
eruption	**uitbarsting**	[œitbarstiŋ]
lava	**lawa**	[lava]
twister, tornado	**tornado**	[tornado]
typhoon	**tifoon**	[tifoən]
hurricane	**orkaan**	[orkān]
storm	**storm**	[storm]
tsunami	**tsunami**	[tsunami]
cyclone	**sikloon**	[sikloən]
bad weather	**slegte weer**	[sleχtə veər]
fire (accident)	**brand**	[brant]
disaster	**ramp**	[ramp]
meteorite	**meteoriet**	[meteorit]
avalanche	**lawine**	[lavinə]
snowslide	**sneeulawine**	[sniʊ·lavinə]
blizzard	**sneeustorm**	[sniʊ·storm]
snowstorm	**sneeustorm**	[sniʊ·storm]

Fauna

174. Mammals. Predators

predator	**roofdier**	[roəf·dir]
tiger	**tier**	[tir]
lion	**leeu**	[liʊ]
wolf	**wolf**	[volf]
fox	**vos**	[fos]
jaguar	**jaguar**	[jaχuar]
leopard	**luiperd**	[lœipert]
cheetah	**jagluiperd**	[jaχ·lœipert]
black panther	**swart luiperd**	[swart lœipert]
puma	**poema**	[puma]
snow leopard	**sneeuluiperd**	[sniʊ·lœipert]
lynx	**los**	[los]
coyote	**prêriewolf**	[præri·volf]
jackal	**jakkals**	[jakkals]
hyena	**hiëna**	[hiɛna]

175. Wild animals

animal	**dier**	[dir]
beast (animal)	**beest**	[beəst]
squirrel	**eekhoring**	[eəkhoriŋ]
hedgehog	**krimpvarkie**	[krimpfarki]
hare	**hasie**	[hasi]
rabbit	**konyn**	[konajn]
badger	**das**	[das]
raccoon	**wasbeer**	[vasbeər]
hamster	**hamster**	[hamstər]
marmot	**marmot**	[marmot]
mole	**mol**	[mol]
mouse	**muis**	[mœis]
rat	**rot**	[rot]
bat	**vlermuis**	[fler·mœis]
ermine	**hermelyn**	[herməlajn]
sable	**sabel, sabeldier**	[sabəl], [sabəl·dir]
marten	**marter**	[martər]
weasel	**wesel**	[vesəl]
mink	**nerts**	[nerts]

| beaver | bewer | [bevər] |
| otter | otter | [ottər] |

horse	perd	[pert]
moose	eland	[ɛlant]
deer	hert	[hert]
camel	kameel	[kameəl]

bison	bison	[bison]
wisent	wisent	[visent]
buffalo	buffel	[buffəl]

zebra	sebra, kwagga	[sebra], [kwaχχa]
antelope	wildsbok	[vilds·bok]
roe deer	reebok	[reəbok]
fallow deer	damhert	[damhert]
chamois	gems	[χems]
wild boar	wildevark	[vildə·fark]

whale	walvis	[valfis]
seal	seehond	[seə·hont]
walrus	walrus	[valrus]
fur seal	seebeer	[seə·beər]
dolphin	dolfyn	[dolfajn]

bear	beer	[beər]
polar bear	ysbeer	[ajs·beər]
panda	panda	[panda]

monkey	aap	[ãp]
chimpanzee	sjimpansee	[ʃimpaŋseə]
orangutan	orangoetang	[oranχutaŋ]
gorilla	gorilla	[χorilla]
macaque	makaak	[makāk]
gibbon	gibbon	[χibbon]

elephant	olifant	[olifant]
rhinoceros	renoster	[renostər]
giraffe	kameelperd	[kameəl·pert]
hippopotamus	seekoei	[seə·kui]

| kangaroo | kangaroe | [kanχaru] |
| koala (bear) | koala | [koala] |

mongoose	muishond	[mœis·hont]
chinchilla	chinchilla, tjintjilla	[tʃin·tʃila]
skunk	stinkmuishond	[stinkmœis·hont]
porcupine	ystervark	[ajstər·fark]

176. Domestic animals

cat	kat	[kat]
tomcat	kater	[katər]
dog	hond	[hont]

horse	**perd**	[pert]
stallion (male horse)	**hings**	[hiŋs]
mare	**merrie**	[merri]
cow	**koei**	[kui]
bull	**bul**	[bul]
ox	**os**	[os]
sheep (ewe)	**skaap**	[skāp]
ram	**ram**	[ram]
goat	**bok**	[bok]
billy goat, he-goat	**bokram**	[bok·ram]
donkey	**donkie, esel**	[donki], [eisəl]
mule	**muil**	[mœil]
pig	**vark**	[fark]
piglet	**varkie**	[farki]
rabbit	**konyn**	[konajn]
hen (chicken)	**hoender, hen**	[hundər], [hen]
cock	**haan**	[hān]
duck	**eend**	[eent]
drake	**mannetjieseend**	[mannəkis·eent]
goose	**gans**	[χaŋs]
tom turkey, gobbler	**kalkoenmannetjie**	[kalkun·mannəki]
turkey (hen)	**kalkoen**	[kalkun]
domestic animals	**huisdiere**	[hœis·dirə]
tame (e.g. ~ hamster)	**mak**	[mak]
to tame (vt)	**mak maak**	[mak māk]
to breed (vt)	**teel**	[teəl]
farm	**plaas**	[plās]
poultry	**pluimvee**	[plœimfeə]
cattle	**beeste**	[beəstə]
herd (cattle)	**kudde**	[kuddə]
stable	**stal**	[stal]
pigsty	**varkstal**	[fark·stal]
cowshed	**koeistal**	[kui·stal]
rabbit hutch	**konynehok**	[konajnə·hok]
hen house	**hoenderhok**	[hundər·hok]

177. Dogs. Dog breeds

dog	**hond**	[hont]
sheepdog	**herdershond**	[herdərs·hont]
German shepherd	**Duitse herdershond**	[dœitsə herdərs·hont]
poodle	**poedel**	[pudəl]
dachshund	**worshond**	[vors·hont]
bulldog	**bulhond**	[bul·hont]

boxer	bokser	[boksər]
mastiff	mastiff	[mastif]
Rottweiler	Rottweiler	[rottwæjlər]
Doberman	Dobermann	[dobermann]

basset	basset	[basset]
bobtail	bobtail	[bobtajl]
Dalmatian	Dalmatiese hond	[dalmatisə hont]
cocker spaniel	sniphond	[snip·hont]

| Newfoundland | Newfoundlander | [njufæʊntlandər] |
| Saint Bernard | Sint Bernard | [sint bernart] |

husky	poolhond, husky	[pulhont], [huski]
Chow Chow	chowchow	[tʃau·tʃau]
spitz	spitshond	[spits·hont]
pug	mopshond	[mops·hont]

178. Sounds made by animals

barking (n)	geblaf	[χeblaf]
to bark (vi)	blaf	[blaf]
to miaow (vi)	miaau	[miãu]
to purr (vi)	spin	[spin]

to moo (vi)	loei	[lui]
to bellow (bull)	bulk	[bulk]
to growl (vi)	grom	[χrom]

howl (n)	gehuil	[χehœil]
to howl (vi)	huil	[hœil]
to whine (vi)	tjank	[tʃank]

to bleat (sheep)	blêr	[blær]
to oink, to grunt (pig)	snork	[snork]
to squeal (vi)	gil	[χil]

to croak (vi)	kwaak	[kwãk]
to buzz (insect)	zoem	[zum]
to chirp (crickets, grasshopper)	kriek	[krik]

179. Birds

bird	voël	[foɛl]
pigeon	duif	[dœif]
sparrow	mossie	[mossi]
tit (great tit)	mees	[meəs]
magpie	ekster	[ɛkstər]

| raven | raaf | [rãf] |
| crow | kraai | [krãi] |

jackdaw	**kerkkraai**	[kerk·krãi]
rook	**roek**	[ruk]
duck	**eend**	[eent]
goose	**gans**	[χaŋs]
pheasant	**fisant**	[fisant]
eagle	**arend**	[arɛnt]
hawk	**sperwer**	[sperwər]
falcon	**valk**	[falk]
vulture	**aasvoël**	[āsfoɛl]
condor (Andean ~)	**kondor**	[kondor]
swan	**swaan**	[swãn]
crane	**kraanvoël**	[krãn·foɛl]
stork	**ooievaar**	[ojefãr]
parrot	**papegaai**	[papəχãi]
hummingbird	**kolibrie**	[kolibri]
peacock	**pou**	[pæʊ]
ostrich	**volstruis**	[folstrœis]
heron	**reier**	[ræjer]
flamingo	**flamink**	[flamink]
pelican	**pelikaan**	[pelikãn]
nightingale	**nagtegaal**	[naχteχãl]
swallow	**swael**	[swaəl]
thrush	**lyster**	[lajstər]
song thrush	**sanglyster**	[saŋlajstər]
blackbird	**merel**	[merəl]
swift	**windswael**	[vindswaəl]
lark	**lewerik**	[leverik]
quail	**kwartel**	[kwartəl]
woodpecker	**speg**	[speχ]
cuckoo	**koekoek**	[kukuk]
owl	**uil**	[œil]
eagle owl	**ooruil**	[oərœil]
wood grouse	**auerhoen**	[ɔuer·hun]
black grouse	**korhoen**	[korhun]
partridge	**patrys**	[patrajs]
starling	**spreeu**	[spriʊ]
canary	**kanarie**	[kanari]
hazel grouse	**bonasa hoen**	[bonasa hun]
chaffinch	**gryskoppie**	[χrajskoppi]
bullfinch	**bloedvink**	[bludfink]
seagull	**seemeeu**	[seəmiʊ]
albatross	**albatros**	[albatros]
penguin	**pikkewyn**	[pikkəvajn]

180. Birds. Singing and sounds

to sing (vi)	fluit	[flœit]
to call (animal, bird)	roep	[rup]
to crow (cock)	kraai	[krāi]
cock-a-doodle-doo	koekelekoe	[kukeleku]
to cluck (hen)	kekkel	[kɛkkəl]
to caw (crow call)	kras	[kras]
to quack (duck call)	kwaak	[kwāk]
to cheep (vi)	piep	[pip]
to chirp, to twitter	tjilp	[ʧilp]

181. Fish. Marine animals

bream	brasem	[brasem]
carp	karp	[karp]
perch	baars	[bārs]
catfish	katvis, seebaber	[katfis], [see·babər]
pike	snoek	[snuk]
salmon	salm	[salm]
sturgeon	steur	[støør]
herring	haring	[hariŋ]
Atlantic salmon	atlantiese salm	[atlantisə salm]
mackerel	makriel	[makril]
flatfish	platvis	[platfis]
zander, pike perch	varswatersnoek	[farswatər·snuk]
cod	kabeljou	[kabeljæʊ]
tuna	tuna	[tuna]
trout	forel	[forəl]
eel	paling	[paliŋ]
electric ray	drilvis	[drilfis]
moray eel	bontpaling	[bontpaliŋ]
piranha	piranha	[piranha]
shark	haai	[hāi]
dolphin	dolfyn	[dolfajn]
whale	walvis	[valfis]
crab	krap	[krap]
jellyfish	jellievis	[jelli·fis]
octopus	seekat	[see·kat]
starfish	seester	[see·stər]
sea urchin	see-egel, seekastaiing	[see-eҳel], [see·kastajiŋ]
seahorse	seeperdjie	[see·perdʒi]
oyster	oester	[ustər]
prawn	garnaal	[ҳarnāl]

| lobster | kreef | [kreəf] |
| spiny lobster | seekreef | [seə·kreəf] |

182. Amphibians. Reptiles

| snake | slang | [slaŋ] |
| venomous (snake) | giftig | [χiftəχ] |

viper	adder	[addər]
cobra	kobra	[kobra]
python	luislang	[lœislaŋ]
boa	boa, konstriktorslang	[boa], [koŋstriktor·slaŋ]

grass snake	ringslang	[riŋ·slaŋ]
rattle snake	ratelslang	[ratəl·slaŋ]
anaconda	anakonda	[anakonda]

lizard	akkedis	[akkedis]
iguana	leguaan	[leχuān]
monitor lizard	likkewaan	[likkevān]
salamander	salamander	[salamandər]
chameleon	verkleurmannetjie	[fərkløər·manneki]
scorpion	skerpioen	[skerpiun]

turtle	skilpad	[skilpat]
frog	padda	[padda]
toad	brulpadda	[brul·padda]
crocodile	krokodil	[krokodil]

183. Insects

insect	insek	[insek]
butterfly	skoenlapper	[skunlappər]
ant	mier	[mir]
fly	vlieg	[fliχ]
mosquito	muskiet	[muskit]
beetle	kewer	[kevər]

wasp	perdeby	[perdə·baj]
bee	by	[baj]
bumblebee	hommelby	[homməl·baj]
gadfly (botfly)	perdevlieg	[perdə·fliχ]

| spider | spinnekop | [spinnə·kop] |
| spider's web | spinnerak | [spinnə·rak] |

dragonfly	naaldekoker	[nāldə·kokər]
grasshopper	sprinkaan	[sprinkān]
moth (night butterfly)	mot	[mot]

| cockroach | kakkerlak | [kakkerlak] |
| tick | bosluis | [boslœis] |

| flea | vlooi | [floj] |
| midge | muggie | [muχχi] |

locust	treksprinkhaan	[trek·sprinkhãn]
snail	slak	[slak]
cricket	kriek	[krik]
firefly	vuurvliegie	[fɪrfliχi]
ladybird	lieweheersbesie	[liveheərs·besi]
cockchafer	lentekewer	[lentekevər]

leech	bloedsuier	[blud·sœiər]
caterpillar	ruspe	[ruspə]
earthworm	erdwurm	[ɛrd·vurm]
larva	larwe	[larvə]

184. Animals. Body parts

beak	snawel	[snavəl]
wings	vlerke	[flerkə]
foot (of the bird)	poot	[poət]
feathers (plumage)	vere	[ferə]
feather	veer	[feər]
crest	kuif	[kœif]

gills	kiewe	[kivə]
spawn	viseiers	[fisæejers]
larva	larwe	[larvə]
fin	vin	[fin]
scales (of fish, reptile)	skubbe	[skubbə]

fang (canine)	slagtand	[slaχtant]
paw (e.g. cat's ~)	poot	[poət]
muzzle (snout)	muil	[mœil]
mouth (cat's ~)	bek	[bek]
tail	stert	[stert]
whiskers	snor	[snor]

| hoof | hoef | [huf] |
| horn | horing | [horiŋ] |

carapace	rugdop	[ruχdop]
shell (mollusk ~)	skulp	[skulp]
eggshell	eierdop	[æejer·dop]

| animal's hair (pelage) | pels | [pɛls] |
| pelt (hide) | vel | [fəl] |

185. Animals. Habitats

habitat	habitat	[habitat]
migration	migrasie	[miχrasi]
mountain	berg	[berχ]

reef	**rif**	[rif]
cliff	**rots**	[rots]
forest	**woud**	[væʊt]
jungle	**oerwoud**	[urwæʊt]
savanna	**veld**	[fɛlt]
tundra	**toendra**	[tundra]
steppe	**steppe**	[stɛppə]
desert	**woestyn**	[vustajn]
oasis	**oase**	[oasə]
sea	**see**	[seə]
lake	**meer**	[meər]
ocean	**oseaan**	[oseãn]
swamp (marshland)	**moeras**	[muras]
freshwater (adj)	**varswater**	[fars·vatər]
pond	**dam**	[dam]
river	**rivier**	[rifir]
den (bear's ~)	**hol**	[hol]
nest	**nes**	[nes]
tree hollow	**holte**	[holtə]
burrow (animal hole)	**gat**	[ɣat]
anthill	**miershoop**	[mirs·hoəp]

Flora

tree	boom	[boəm]
deciduous (adj)	bladwisselend	[bladwisselent]
coniferous (adj)	kegeldraend	[keχɛldraent]
evergreen (adj)	immergroen	[immərχrun]

apple tree	appelboom	[appɛl·boəm]
pear tree	peerboom	[peer·boəm]
cherry tree	kersieboom	[kersi·boəm]
sweet cherry tree	soetkersieboom	[sutkersi·boəm]
sour cherry tree	suurkersieboom	[sɪrkersi·boəm]
plum tree	pruimeboom	[prœimə·boəm]

birch	berk	[berk]
oak	eik	[æjk]
linden tree	lindeboom	[lində·boəm]

| aspen | trilpopulier | [trilpopulir] |
| maple | esdoring | [ɛsdoriŋ] |

spruce	spar	[spar]
pine	denneboom	[dɛnnə·boəm]
larch	lorkeboom	[lorkə·boəm]

| fir tree | den | [den] |
| cedar | seder | [sedər] |

| poplar | populier | [populir] |
| rowan | lysterbessie | [lajstərbɛssi] |

| willow | wilger | [vilχər] |
| alder | els | [ɛls] |

| beech | beuk | [bøək] |
| elm | olm | [olm] |

| ash (tree) | esboom | [ɛs·boəm] |
| chestnut | kastaiing | [kastajiŋ] |

magnolia	magnolia	[maχnolia]
palm tree	palm	[palm]
cypress	sipres	[sipres]

mangrove	wortelboom	[vortəl·boəm]
baobab	kremetart	[kremetart]
eucalyptus	bloekom	[blukom]
sequoia	mammoetboom	[mammut·boəm]

187. Shrubs

bush	**struik**	[strœik]
shrub	**bossie**	[bossi]
grapevine	**wingerdstok**	[viŋərd·stok]
vineyard	**wingerd**	[viŋərt]
raspberry bush	**framboosstruik**	[framboəs·strœik]
blackcurrant bush	**swartbessiestruik**	[swartbɛssi·strœik]
redcurrant bush	**rooi aalbessiestruik**	[roj ālbɛssi·strœik]
gooseberry bush	**appelliefiestruik**	[appɛllifi·strœik]
acacia	**akasia**	[akasia]
barberry	**suurbessie**	[sɪr·bɛssi]
jasmine	**jasmyn**	[jasmajn]
juniper	**jenewer**	[jenevər]
rosebush	**roosstruik**	[roəs·strœik]
dog rose	**hondsroos**	[honds·roəs]

188. Mushrooms

mushroom	**paddastoel**	[paddastul]
edible mushroom	**eetbare paddastoel**	[eətbarə paddastul]
poisonous mushroom	**giftige paddastoel**	[χiftiχə paddastul]
cap	**hoed**	[hut]
stipe	**steel**	[steəl]
cep, penny bun	**Eetbare boleet**	[eətbarə boleət]
orange-cap boletus	**rooihoed**	[rojhut]
birch bolete	**berkboleet**	[berk·boleət]
chanterelle	**dooierswam**	[dojer·swam]
russula	**russula**	[russula]
morel	**morielje**	[morilje]
fly agaric	**vlieëswam**	[fliɛ·swam]
death cap	**duiwelsbrood**	[dœivɛls·broət]

189. Fruits. Berries

fruit	**vrug**	[fruχ]
fruits	**vrugte**	[fruχtə]
apple	**appel**	[appəl]
pear	**peer**	[peər]
plum	**pruim**	[prœim]
strawberry (garden ~)	**aarbei**	[ārbæj]
cherry	**kersie**	[kersi]
sour cherry	**suurkersie**	[sɪr·kersi]

| sweet cherry | soetkersie | [sut·kersi] |
| grape | druif | [drœif] |

raspberry	framboos	[frambɔəs]
blackcurrant	swartbessie	[swartbɛssi]
redcurrant	rooi aalbessie	[roj ālbɛssi]
gooseberry	appelliefie	[appɛllifi]
cranberry	bosbessie	[bosbɛssi]

orange	lemoen	[lemun]
tangerine	nartjie	[narki]
pineapple	pynappel	[pajnappəl]
banana	piesang	[pisaŋ]
date	dadel	[dadəl]

lemon	suurlemoen	[sɪr·lemun]
apricot	appelkoos	[appɛlkɔəs]
peach	perske	[perskə]
kiwi	kiwi, kiwivrug	[kivi], [kivi·fruχ]
grapefruit	pomelo	[pomelo]

berry	bessie	[bɛssi]
berries	bessies	[bɛssis]
cowberry	pryselbessie	[prajsɛlbɛssi]
wild strawberry	wilde aarbei	[vildə ārbæj]
bilberry	bloubessie	[blæʋbɛssi]

190. Flowers. Plants

| flower | blom | [blom] |
| bouquet (of flowers) | boeket | [buket] |

rose (flower)	roos	[rɔəs]
tulip	tulp	[tulp]
carnation	angelier	[anχəlir]
gladiolus	swaardlelie	[swārd·leli]

cornflower	koringblom	[koriŋblom]
harebell	grasklokkie	[χras·klokki]
dandelion	perdeblom	[perdə·blom]
camomile	kamille	[kamillə]

aloe	aalwyn	[ālwajn]
cactus	kaktus	[kaktus]
rubber plant, ficus	rubberplant	[rubbər·plant]

lily	lelie	[leli]
geranium	malva	[malfa]
hyacinth	hiasint	[hiasint]

mimosa	mimosa	[mimosa]
narcissus	narsing	[narsiŋ]
nasturtium	kappertjie	[kapperki]
orchid	orgidee	[orχideə]

| peony | pinksterroos | [pinkstər·roəs] |
| violet | viooltjie | [fioəlki] |

pansy	gesiggie	[ɣesiχi]
forget-me-not	vergeet-my-nietjie	[ferχeət-maj-niki]
daisy	madeliefie	[madelifi]

poppy	papawer	[papavər]
hemp	hennep	[hɛnnəp]
mint	kruisement	[krœisəment]

| lily of the valley | dallelie | [dalleli] |
| snowdrop | sneeuklokkie | [sniʊ·klokki] |

nettle	brandnetel	[brant·netəl]
sorrel	veldsuring	[fɛltsuriŋ]
water lily	waterlelie	[vatər·leli]
fern	varing	[fariŋ]
lichen	korsmos	[korsmos]

conservatory (greenhouse)	broeikas	[bruikas]
lawn	grasperk	[χras·perk]
flowerbed	blombed	[blom·bet]

plant	plant	[plant]
grass	gras	[χras]
blade of grass	grasspriet	[χras·sprit]

leaf	blaar	[blãr]
petal	kroonblaar	[kroən·blãr]
stem	stingel	[stiŋəl]
tuber	knol	[knol]

| young plant (shoot) | saailing | [sãjliŋ] |
| thorn | doring | [doriŋ] |

to blossom (vi)	bloei	[blui]
to fade, to wither	verlep	[ferlep]
smell (odour)	reuk	[røək]
to cut (flowers)	sny	[snaj]
to pick (a flower)	pluk	[pluk]

191. Cereals, grains

grain	graan	[χrãn]
cereal crops	graangewasse	[χrãn·χəwassə]
ear (of barley, etc.)	aar	[ãr]

wheat	koring	[koriŋ]
rye	rog	[roχ]
oats	hawer	[havər]
millet	gierst	[χirst]
barley	gars	[χars]
maize	mielie	[mili]

| rice | **rys** | [rajs] |
| buckwheat | **bokwiet** | [bokwit] |

pea plant	**ertjie**	[ɛrki]
kidney bean	**nierboon**	[nir·boən]
soya	**soja**	[soja]
lentil	**lensie**	[lɛŋsi]
beans (pulse crops)	**boontjies**	[boənkis]

REGIONAL GEOGRAPHY

192. Politics. Government. Part 1

politics	politiek	[politik]
political (adj)	politieke	[politikə]
politician	politikus	[politikus]

state (country)	staat	[stāt]
citizen	burger	[burgər]
citizenship	burgerskap	[burgərskap]

| national emblem | nasionale wapen | [naʃionalə vapen] |
| national anthem | volkslied | [folkslit] |

government	regering	[reχeriŋ]
head of state	staatshoof	[stāts·hoəf]
parliament	parlement	[parlement]
party	partij	[partij]

| capitalism | kapitalisme | [kapitalismə] |
| capitalist (adj) | kapitalis | [kapitalis] |

| socialism | sosialisme | [soʃialisme] |
| socialist (adj) | sosialis | [soʃialis] |

communism	kommunisme	[kommunismə]
communist (adj)	kommunis	[kommunis]
communist (n)	kommunis	[kommunis]

democracy	demokrasie	[demokrasi]
democrat	demokraat	[demokrāt]
democratic (adj)	demokraties	[demokratis]
Democratic party	Demokratiese party	[demokratisə partaj]

| liberal (n) | liberaal | [liberāl] |
| Liberal (adj) | liberaal | [liberāl] |

| conservative (n) | konservatief | [kɔŋserfatif] |
| conservative (adj) | konservatief | [kɔŋserfatif] |

republic (n)	republiek	[republik]
republican (n)	republikein	[republikæjn]
Republican party	Republikeinse Party	[republikæjnsə partaj]

elections	verkiesings	[ferkisiŋs]
to elect (vt)	verkies	[ferkis]
elector, voter	kieser	[kisər]
election campaign	verkiesingskampanje	[ferkisiŋs·kampanje]
voting (n)	stemming	[stɛmmiŋ]

| to vote (vi) | stem | [stem] |
| suffrage, right to vote | stemreg | [stem·reχ] |

| candidate | kandidaat | [kandidāt] |
| campaign | kampanje | [kampanje] |

| opposition (as adj) | opposisie | [opposisi] |
| opposition (n) | opposisie | [opposisi] |

visit	besoek	[besuk]
official visit	amptelike besoek	[amptelikə besuk]
international (adj)	internasionaal	[internaʃionāl]

| negotiations | onderhandelinge | [ondərhandeliŋə] |
| to negotiate (vi) | onderhandel | [ondərhandəl] |

193. Politics. Government. Part 2

society	samelewing	[sameleviŋ]
constitution	grondwet	[χront·wet]
power (political control)	mag	[maχ]
corruption	korrupsie	[korrupsi]

| law (justice) | wet | [vet] |
| legal (legitimate) | wetlik | [vetlik] |

| justice (fairness) | geregtigheid | [χereχtiχæjt] |
| just (fair) | regverdig | [reχferdəχ] |

committee	komitee	[komiteə]
bill (draft law)	wetsontwerp	[vetsontwerp]
budget	begroting	[beχrotiŋ]
policy	beleid	[belæjt]
reform	hervorming	[herformiŋ]
radical (adj)	radikaal	[radikāl]

power (strength, force)	mag	[maχ]
powerful (adj)	magtig	[maχtəχ]
supporter	ondersteuner	[ondərstøənər]
influence	invloed	[influt]

regime (e.g. military ~)	bewind	[bevint]
conflict	konflik	[konflik]
conspiracy (plot)	sameswering	[samesweriŋ]
provocation	uitdaging	[œitdaχiŋ]

to overthrow (regime, etc.)	omvergooi	[omferχoj]
overthrow (of a government)	omvergooi	[omferχoj]
revolution	revolusie	[refolusi]

coup d'état	staatsgreep	[stāts·χreəp]
military coup	militêre staatsgreep	[militærə stātsχreəp]
crisis	krisis	[krisis]
economic recession	ekonomiese agteruitgang	[ɛkonomisə aχtər·œitχaŋ]

demonstrator (protester)	betoër	[betoɛr]
demonstration	demonstrasie	[demɔŋstrasi]
martial law	krygswet	[krajχs·wet]
military base	militêre basis	[militæːrə basis]

| stability | stabiliteit | [stabilitæjt] |
| stable (adj) | stabiel | [stabil] |

| exploitation | uitbuiting | [œitbœitiŋ] |
| to exploit (workers) | uitbuit | [œitbœit] |

racism	rassisme	[rassismə]
racist	rassis	[rassis]
fascism	fascisme	[faʃismə]
fascist	fascis	[faʃis]

194. Countries. Miscellaneous

foreigner	vreemdeling	[freəmdeliŋ]
foreign (adj)	vreemd	[freəmt]
abroad (in a foreign country)	in die buiteland	[in di bœitəlant]

emigrant	emigrant	[ɛmiχrant]
emigration	emigrasie	[ɛmiχrasi]
to emigrate (vi)	emigreer	[ɛmiχreər]

the West	die Weste	[di vestə]
the East	die Ooste	[di oəstə]
the Far East	die Verre Ooste	[di ferrə oəstə]

civilization	beskawing	[beskaviŋ]
humanity (mankind)	mensdom	[mɛŋsdom]
the world (earth)	die wêreld	[di væːrəlt]
peace	vrede	[fredə]
worldwide (adj)	wêreldwyd	[væːrəlt·wajt]

homeland	vaderland	[fadər·lant]
people (population)	volk	[folk]
population	bevolking	[befolkiŋ]
people (a lot of ~)	mense	[mɛŋsə]
nation (people)	nasie	[nasi]
generation	generasie	[χenerasi]

territory (area)	gebied	[χebit]
region	streek	[streək]
state (part of a country)	staat	[stãt]

tradition	tradisie	[tradisi]
custom (tradition)	gebruik	[χebrœik]
ecology	ekologie	[ɛkoloχi]

Indian (Native American)	Indiaan	[indiãn]
Gypsy (masc.)	Sigeuner	[siχøənər]
Gypsy (fem.)	Sigeunerin	[siχøənərin]

Gypsy (adj)	sigeuner-	[siχøənər-]
empire	rijk	[rijk]
colony	kolonie	[koloni]
slavery	slawerny	[slavərnaj]
invasion	invasie	[infasi]
famine	hongersnood	[hoŋərsnoət]

195. Major religious groups. Confessions

| religion | godsdiens | [χodsdiŋs] |
| religious (adj) | godsdienstig | [χodsdiŋstəχ] |

faith, belief	geloof	[χeloəf]
to believe (in God)	glo	[χlo]
believer	gelowige	[χeloviχə]

| atheism | ateïsme | [ateïsmə] |
| atheist | ateïs | [ateïs] |

Christianity	Christendom	[χristəndom]
Christian (n)	Christen	[χristən]
Christian (adj)	Christelik	[χristəlik]

Catholicism	Katolisisme	[katolisismə]
Catholic (n)	Katoliek	[katolik]
Catholic (adj)	katoliek	[katolik]

Protestantism	Protestantisme	[protestantismə]
Protestant Church	Protestantse Kerk	[protestantsə kerk]
Protestant (n)	Protestant	[protestant]

Orthodoxy	Ortodoksie	[ortodoksi]
Orthodox Church	Ortodokse Kerk	[ortodoksə kerk]
Orthodox (n)	Ortodoks	[ortodoks]

Presbyterianism	Presbiterianisme	[presbiterianismə]
Presbyterian Church	Presbiteriaanse Kerk	[presbiteriãŋsə kerk]
Presbyterian (n)	Presbiteriaan	[presbitəriãn]

| Lutheranism | Lutheranisme | [luteranismə] |
| Lutheran (n) | Lutheraan | [lutərãn] |

| Baptist Church | Baptistiese Kerk | [baptistisə kerk] |
| Baptist (n) | Baptis | [baptis] |

| Anglican Church | Anglikaanse Kerk | [anχlikãŋsə kerk] |
| Anglican (n) | Anglikaan | [anχlikãn] |

| Mormonism | Mormonisme | [mormonismə] |
| Mormon (n) | Mormoon | [mormoən] |

Judaism	Jodendom	[jodɛndom]
Jew (n)	Jood	[joət]
Buddhism	Boeddhisme	[buddismə]

Buddhist (n)	**Boeddhis**	[buddis]
Hinduism	**Hindoeïsme**	[hinduïsmə]
Hindu (n)	**Hindoe**	[hindu]
Islam	**Islam**	[islam]
Muslim (n)	**Islamiet**	[islamit]
Muslim (adj)	**Islamities**	[islamitis]
Shiah Islam	**Sjia Islam**	[ʃia islam]
Shiite (n)	**Sjiït**	[ʃiït]
Sunni Islam	**Sunni Islam**	[sunni islam]
Sunnite (n)	**Sunniet**	[sunnit]

196. Religions. Priests

priest	**priester**	[pristər]
the Pope	**die Pous**	[di pæus]
monk, friar	**monnik**	[monnik]
nun	**non**	[non]
pastor	**pastoor**	[pastoər]
abbot	**ab**	[ap]
vicar (parish priest)	**priester**	[pristər]
bishop	**biskop**	[biskop]
cardinal	**kardinaal**	[kardinãl]
preacher	**predikant**	[predikant]
preaching	**preek**	[preək]
parishioners	**kerkgangers**	[kerk·xaŋərs]
believer	**gelowige**	[xelovixə]
atheist	**ateïs**	[ateïs]

197. Faith. Christianity. Islam

Adam	**Adam**	[adam]
Eve	**Eva**	[efa]
God	**God**	[xot]
the Lord	**die Here**	[di herə]
the Almighty	**die Almagtige**	[di almaxtixə]
sin	**sonde**	[sondə]
to sin (vi)	**sondig**	[sondəx]
sinner (masc.)	**sondaar**	[sondãr]
sinner (fem.)	**sondares**	[sondares]
hell	**hel**	[həl]
paradise	**paradys**	[paradajs]
Jesus	**Jesus**	[jesus]

Jesus Christ	Jesus Christus	[jesus χristus]
the Holy Spirit	die Heilige Gees	[di hæjliχə χees]
the Saviour	die Verlosser	[di ferlossər]
the Virgin Mary	die Maagd Maria	[di mãχt maria]

the Devil	die duiwel	[di dœivəl]
devil's (adj)	duiwels	[dœivɛls]
Satan	Satan	[satan]
satanic (adj)	satanies	[satanis]

angel	engel	[ɛŋəl]
guardian angel	beskermengel	[beskerm·eŋəl]
angelic (adj)	engelagtig	[ɛŋəlaχtəχ]

apostle	apostel	[apostəl]
archangel	aartsengel	[ãrtseŋəl]
the Antichrist	die antichris	[di antiχris]

Church	Kerk	[kerk]
Bible	Bybel	[bajbəl]
biblical (adj)	bybels	[bajbəls]

Old Testament	Ou Testament	[æʊ testament]
New Testament	Nuwe Testament	[nuvə testament]
Gospel	evangelie	[ɛfanχəli]
Holy Scripture	Heilige Skrif	[hæjliχə skrif]
Heaven	hemel	[heməl]

Commandment	gebod	[χebot]
prophet	profeet	[profeet]
prophecy	profesie	[profesi]

Allah	Allah	[allah]
Mohammed	Mohammed	[mohammet]
the Koran	die Koran	[di koran]

mosque	moskee	[moskeə]
mullah	moella	[mulla]
prayer	gebed	[χebet]
to pray (vi, vt)	bid	[bit]

pilgrimage	pelgrimstog	[pɛlχrimstoχ]
pilgrim	pelgrim	[pɛlχrim]
Mecca	Mecca	[mɛkka]

church	kerk	[kerk]
temple	tempel	[tempəl]
cathedral	katedraal	[katedrãl]
Gothic (adj)	Goties	[χotis]
synagogue	sinagoge	[sinaχoχə]
mosque	moskee	[moskeə]

chapel	kapel	[kapəl]
abbey	abdy	[abdaj]
convent	klooster	[kloəstər]
monastery	klooster	[kloəstər]

bell (church ~s)	klok	[klok]
bell tower	kloktoring	[klok·toriŋ]
to ring (ab. bells)	lui	[lœi]

cross	kruis	[krœis]
cupola (roof)	koepel	[kupəl]
icon	ikoon	[ikoən]

soul	siel	[sil]
fate (destiny)	noodlot	[noədlot]
evil (n)	die bose	[di bosə]
good (n)	goed	[χut]

vampire	vampier	[fampir]
witch (evil ~)	heks	[heks]
demon	demoon	[demoən]
spirit	gees	[χeəs]

| redemption (giving us ~) | versoening | [fersuniŋ] |
| to redeem (vt) | verlos | [ferlos] |

church service	kerkdies	[kerkdis]
to say mass	die mis opdra	[di mis opdra]
confession	bieg	[biχ]
to confess (vi)	bieg	[biχ]

saint (n)	heilige	[hæjliχə]
sacred (holy)	heilig	[hæjləχ]
holy water	wywater	[vaj·vatər]

ritual (n)	ritueel	[ritueəl]
ritual (adj)	ritueel	[ritueəl]
sacrifice	offerande	[offerandə]

superstition	bygeloof	[bajχəloəf]
superstitious (adj)	bygelowig	[bajχəlovəχ]
afterlife	hiernamaals	[hirna·mãls]
eternal life	ewige lewe	[ɛviχə levə]

MISCELLANEOUS

198. Various useful words

background (green ~)	**agtergrond**	[aχtərχront]
balance (of the situation)	**balans**	[balaŋs]
barrier (obstacle)	**hindernis**	[hindərnis]
base (basis)	**basis**	[basis]
beginning	**begin**	[beχin]
category	**kategorie**	[kateχori]
cause (reason)	**rede**	[redə]
choice	**keuse**	[køəsə]
coincidence	**toeval**	[tufal]
comfortable (~ chair)	**gemaklik**	[χemaklik]
comparison	**vergelyking**	[ferχelajkiŋ]
compensation	**kompensasie**	[kompɛnsasi]
degree (extent, amount)	**graad**	[χrãt]
development	**ontwikkeling**	[ontwikkeliŋ]
difference	**verskil**	[ferskil]
effect (e.g. of drugs)	**effek**	[ɛffek]
effort (exertion)	**inspanning**	[inspanniŋ]
element	**element**	[ɛlement]
end (finish)	**einde**	[æjndə]
example (illustration)	**voorbeeld**	[foərbeəlt]
fact	**feit**	[fæjt]
frequent (adj)	**gereeld**	[χereəlt]
growth (development)	**groei**	[χrui]
help	**hulp**	[hulp]
ideal	**ideaal**	[ideãl]
kind (sort, type)	**soort**	[soərt]
labyrinth	**labirint**	[labirint]
mistake, error	**fout**	[fæut]
moment	**moment**	[moment]
object (thing)	**objek**	[objek]
obstacle	**hinderpaal**	[hindərpãl]
original (original copy)	**origineel**	[oriχineəl]
part (~ of sth)	**deel**	[deəl]
particle, small part	**deeltjie**	[deəlki]
pause (break)	**pouse**	[pæusə]
position	**posisie**	[posisi]
principle	**beginsel**	[beχinsəl]
problem	**probleem**	[probleəm]
process	**proses**	[proses]

progress	**vooruitgang**	[foərœeitχaŋ]
property (quality)	**eienskap**	[æjeŋskap]
reaction	**reaksie**	[reaksi]
risk	**risiko**	[risiko]
secret	**geheim**	[χəhæjm]
series	**reeks**	[reəks]
shape (outer form)	**vorm**	[form]
situation	**toestand**	[tustant]
solution	**oplossing**	[oplossiŋ]
standard (adj)	**standaard**	[standãrt]
standard (level of quality)	**standaard**	[standãrt]
stop (pause)	**pouse**	[pæʊsə]
style	**styl**	[stajl]
system	**sisteem**	[sisteəm]
table (chart)	**tabel**	[tabəl]
tempo, rate	**tempo**	[tempo]
term (word, expression)	**term**	[term]
thing (object, item)	**ding**	[diŋ]
truth (e.g. moment of ~)	**waarheid**	[vãrhæjt]
turn (please wait your ~)	**beurt**	[bøərt]
type (sort, kind)	**tipe**	[tipə]
urgent (adj)	**dringend**	[driŋəŋ]
urgently	**dringend**	[driŋəŋ]
utility (usefulness)	**nut**	[nut]
variant (alternative)	**variant**	[fariant]
way (means, method)	**manier**	[manir]
zone	**sone**	[sonə]